EXPLORING ATLANTIS
Volume III

DR. FRANK ALPER

ARIZONA METAPHYSICAL SOCIETY
P.O. BOX 44027, PHOENIX, AZ 85064

ISBN No. 0-929365-03-8

Contents

* * FROM THE HEART OF FRANK * *

We wish to remind all that what is written here relates to spiritual healing. All depends on your faith in God. There are no guarantees, no promises, only your own spiritual belief. Bless you.

Introduction

This book is the completion of a trilogy of spiritual channelings concerning the use of quartz crystals and the civilization of Atlantis.

We have been Blessed by the energies of "Strength" from Atlantis, Kryon, Creation, Atemose II, Pythagoras, and Our soul Adamis.

Through these linkages, we have brought forth the information contained in the three volumes. There has been no research or study involved, only the faith in God.

We dedicate this trilogy to all spirit within Our sphere of reception for having faith and trust in Us to serve in Our truth.

We Bless Bishop Amy Kees and Bishop Dorothe Blackmere, the founders of the Church of Tzaddi, for providing a spiritual haven for Children searching for God.

We Bless Our wife, Helene Laura, for her support and faith during the many years of Our struggle to find Our soul. Frank and Adamis are as One. We Bless you, one and all.

*We speak to you tonight as Atemose II,
Ruler of Atlantis. Blessings to you.*

*We begin the final leg of the triangle. We are
going to create the trinity of expressions that,
it is hoped, will be made available to mankind
during your times—a completed picture
of the causes and effects that were created
through the existence of ancient Atlantis.*

A MORE COMPLETE PICTURE OF ATLANTIS

When the city of Atlantis was to be rebuilt, after
the changes had occurred upon the surface of this planet,
those souls who were needed to incarnate there for
areas of service, reconstruction, and restoration did so
under an entirely voluntary system. Yet there were many
who incarnated in Atlantis partially against their will
and desire, but doing so because they did not wish to
offend the Father. They knew that it was their responsibility, because of the nature of their knowledge and
energies, to serve where they were called upon.

Mankind has romantically portrayed a beautiful
picture of the civilizations in Atlantis, depicting it as an
ideal society, with no serious problems, with everyone

living in harmony and unison and working toward a common goal. Perhaps if we look at the overall accomplishments of that time, it is natural to come to this conclusion. However, we must look beneath the surface. We must look into the souls of those who existed there during those times. When we do this, we find many who did not live in their truth, who did not express themselves in their truth. For this reason, at various times during their incarnations, they took actions that were improper—improper for them on a personal level, and improper in relation to their service for God.

It has been said to you many times that history always repeats itself, and this is, of course, quite true. If you look at your world at the present time and throughout the course of its history, you can see great similarities in attitudes and behavior to those of certain segments of the Atlanteans. The struggles for power, for control of others; the development of weaponry, of power sources to establish control militarily and personally; your modern-day experiments with life, with attempts to clone images of yourselves to create Aryan, or pure specimens of mankind—are any of these any different from the Atlantean creation of mutations, any different from the devious experiments that were conducted?

In the end, the Atlanteans were destroyed. In the end of your segment of history, those same vibrations must also be destroyed. However, the method of destruction does not necessarily have to be the same. The object is that mankind must learn from its past actions. It must learn that it need not suffer this type of destruction, that it can be transmuted. This is what is hoped will occur on the surface of your planet, and to this point, the great leaps in consciousness are occurring, and the coming together is also taking place.

THOSE WHO DEPARTED AND THOSE WHO REMAINED

There were many souls incarnated in Atlantis who perished a watery death and an explosive death when the end came. There were others who were spared this experience, for it was something they had no need to endure, no need to be involved with. What made the distinction? Who determined which souls were to perish a suffering existence and which were to be spared, and why? To answer these questions, think of individuals within your own civilization who, in reaching advanced years, close their eyes during their sleep period and make transition, or endure a stress or rupture of the arteries and pass instantaneously. You say to yourself that those souls were truly blessed, for transition was painless and swift, without suffering. The situation is the same.

It has been written, as you sow so shall you reap. When you take unto yourself burdens, damage to your vibrations, untruths, power, and greed, they must be washed away by waters, burned away by fire. And so there was no one individual who sat with a checklist, deciding who should remain and who would be allowed to leave before the end came. That is just the way it was and always is.

Think of someone you know who may have suffered for years with advanced disease, and yet hung on and on. Look over his lifetime; look into his conscious relationship with God; look into his actions relating to mankind, and the answer will always be there.

THE PLAN FOR RESETTLING EARTH

Those Atlantean Elders who were informed of the imminent destruction of their civilization passed out of the physical plane at all ages, for their responsibility had been completed. And these were among the earliest settlers in physical structure upon the surface of Earth. When the cataclysm had quieted down, it had been decided by the Hierarchy that it was time to resettle the surface of Earth, and these Atlantean Elders were "chosen by God" to resurrect civilizations. What of the others? They remained in spiritual form, subject to reconditioning, to having the aberrations in their energies corrected so that they could follow—and also serve properly—upon the surface of earth.

We have talked of the Garden of Eden. We have talked of the symbolic Adam and Eve and the snake. We have described the relationship to you: the male, the female, the free will, and the planet Earth. You may go back as far as you wish through your New Testament, your Old Testament, your Koran, through innumerable of our writings, and they all relate to the Atlantean Elders here to resettle civilizations upon the surface of Earth. How could it have been otherwise? How could a soul without the strength and evolution of an Ascended Master endure the hardships of an Abraham, an Isaac, a Jacob? How could they have endured unless they knew why they were here, what their function was—unless they knew of the external existence of their souls?

Jacob and his wife bore unto themselves twelve sons. And upon their birth, the balance of the Atlantean Elders began to incarnate upon the surface of the planet. They were here to assist, to learn, to continue to work out the aberrations that they had created for themselves. They incarnated in multitudes and, under the direction of the sons, spread out to the four corners of this planet to begin the process of reconstruction.

Find me a soul who has not, at one point within its existence, denied the existence of God, and I shall find you an angel, one who has never been involved in a physical incarnation. After all, it is part of the imperfections of the soul, and the denial of God must be experienced by a soul in order for it to realize the value of God to its existence. This is merely an example of experiencing what you do not want, in order to help you determine your truth. Once a soul experiences the absence of God, it is aware of its truth.

THE MASTER JESUS

There came a point in the evolution of your history when an Emissary from God incarnated upon the surface of Earth. The Elders were informed of the impending presence of this soul, and they gathered together. When the Soul assumed the place in the physical child, ancient vibrations and reactions rose to the surface. Jealousies manifested themselves. The Elders of Atlantis denied the presence of the Master Jesus within the physical body.

But they knew the truth; they knew who He was, and yet fell back into old patterns, and once again denied the existence of God. They defended their decisions, and they protested that it was not God's Will. But in their souls they knew that it was.

Why did that Master Soul come into physical form? What was the function for these vibrations? After all, they had been present many times before. Why was there a special function at that time, or was there one? It would seem that, during that period of history, the Elders were once again in disarray. Unity was not present. The faith and belief in God was almost on the verge of being strewn to the winds. A force of unity, an expression of power, had been determined to be necessary to walk among mankind. This was done to reunite the bonds of man and God. Do not think for one moment that this event had as its basic function the creation of a new expression or religion, for in no manner was this true.

As is always the case, when the energies for a situation manifest themselves, a corresponding experience and pattern of actions becomes generated. So it came to pass, and an opportunity arose for new lessons for mankind, for new expressions to learn. And the new path to God had begun. What has happened to those Elders of Atlantis who called themselves Hebrews when they denied God? Some historians say that, from that time, the race of Hebrews have suffered and lived as nomads; that they have wandered and been denied their homeland; that they have been persecuted throughout the world; that as a race of people they have been born to suffer, to cleanse themselves of sin. This is, of course, invalid, for there is no sin.

You who are sitting and reading these words are part of these vibrations of rejection. For many, it is part of the reason that you are here now at this time, to learn that there never was a necessity to carry the guilt; that there never was a necessity to punish because of rejection; that it was only the decision of the conscious mind, of the generations of vibrations of guilt that man imposed upon itself.

What of those who crucified this Man? Tell me the difference between the crucifixion of an aspect of God and the slaughter of twelve million people. Is one worse than the other? Could not that aspect of God reach a hundredfold twelve-million? Did not each man, woman, and child die a little bit with that crucifixion, even though some denied that fact? And so it happened once again.

Where does the karma lie? Does it lie on the one man that took the life of one or twelve-million? Or does the karma lie in the balance of mankind who, out of their free will, permitted this to occur? Who has committed the greater "sin"—those who followed their believes, or those who hid their heads in the sand, denying this existence? Mankind is approaching a point today of reviving these ancient vibrations once again. The method is different, for we are not dealing with one individual, with one man or woman. We are dealing with many. There are those in all corners of your world who walk as shepherds, who serve as Messiahs, for what happened in the past will never again occur in the future.

THE COMING TOGETHER

It has been said that there is a coming together of the Atlanteans. There is an awareness, a recognition, a blending taking place—and this is truth. These souls are awakening from their slumber; they are entering incarnations through birth, entering through mature years and younger years by materializing purely from spirit into physical structure; and all are appearing in multitudes. It is the Day of Reckoning. It is the Day of Cleansing. It is time to wipe the slate clean. It is as if God has said, "Enough is enough; there are no more times for games; there are no more times for sitting on the fence feeling sorry for yourself; it is time to acknowledge your truth and put into actions the power of your souls."

So mankind is suddenly faced with a position that it cannot avoid. This is confrontation with all its ancient karma, with the awareness coming through conscious mind of things that must be accomplished that were undone or unresolved during those ancient days.

Can men and women become aware that they can no longer avoid these types of obligations? What effect is this having upon your societies? What effect is this having upon your personal and impersonal relationships? It is having drastic effects. It is as if, in an instant, they become aware that they must cast off what they have taken onto themselves. They become aware that they express themselves in their truth in freedom, without restrictions. They must become aware that they can no longer hide from themselves, for the acceptance must be there. The commitment must be there, for only in this manner can actions follow.

What does this mean, this happening to mankind? Perhaps it is ironic, but in a symbolic manner, all the multitudes that denied that aspect of God thousands of years ago are each undergoing, in varying degrees, their own crucifixion—the facing of the truth, the releasing of all vibrations within their lives. All that is missing is that they are not nailed to a cross. They are being branded with the Universal Star of David, branded with the star that denied the aspect of God, but also the star that is the seed of their origin from the Universe—the star of the creation of Earth. All Atlantean karma is contained within the symbol you refer to as the Star of David, and this is the prime reason. He is among you to soothe you, to love you, to cherish you, so that all of your wounds may be healed.

EFFECTING RELEASE OF ANCIENT COMMITMENTS

The time is coming for mankind to effect a release, a release of all ancient commitments, to bring all of the knowledge from the past to the present, and to use it for the good of mankind; to use it for mankind's growth and development. In the end, all will be most positive in its expression.

It seems like it has taken an awfully long time for

this lesson to be completed. Look at the curve of this experience, and you can see the undulations and fluctuations. You can see the downfall and the risings once again. Each time the downfall has a more shallow curve, and the rising takes place in a shorter period of time. And what is thirty or thirty-five-thousand years when we are dealing with the eternal existence of a soul?

It is time for mankind to connect all of its historical events together, to link them all into the chain that they are part of, to know that, throughout your history, every great event of triumph, as well as of destruction, has been part of a pattern. It is part of a pattern to reclaim for the chosen Children of God. One does not grow by continuouly walking ahead. One wearies and tires and slips back now and then, and in the slipping learns and continues to grow. This has been the evolution of mankind; this has been the smoothing out of the aberrations in the souls of the Elders of Atlantis.

All of those who relate to the vibrations are aware of the true meaning of what we have shared with you, if you allow it to be. If not, it can have a negative expression, but this is not our purpose. We have shared these energies with you for your understanding and for your release. Glory in your Atlantean accomplishments. Be consciously aware and apply the knowledge that is within your souls, so that it can assist mankind. And, in the process, aid your own soul in releasing these ancient karmic patterns.

In this manner, the connection can be severed once and for all time. When that occurs is when Atlantis will have totally arisen. We have shared with you that Atlantis is rising now in your consciousness. It cannot exist in two worlds, only in one. The world of Atlantis that remains beneath the seas is holding back the future Atlantis upon the surface of Earth. You must discern what to bring with you, and you must discern what remains and becomes transmuted. Only you. At times, it will be difficult for you, and difficulties mainly will arise in the expression of your worthiness, your worthiness for these strengths and abilities. You must say to yourself, "They are part of me, and therefore I am them." Always remember that God does not bring you gifts. You develop your abilities through effort, through work, and through faith in your souls. All that God brings you is Its Blessings and Its Love.

THE RISING OF ATLANTIS

We, Atemose II, have walked upon your planet of Earth many times during the course of its existence. We have expressed ourselves upon the planet of Atlantis, upon Atlantis when it existed upon the surface of your Earth prior to the descent. And our vibrations have been present time and time again in later courses of your history. Of all the occasions, perhaps now, at your present time, there is more joy and enthusiasm for mankind.

Upon the twenty-second day of the month of March in your year of 1985, the energies of Atlantis will have totally arisen. Your Aquarian Age will have become in full force and strength. It is a moment in history that has long been awaited. At last it will come to pass. And because of this, without exception, all of those who have served in Atlantis, who have served to resurrect civilizations upon your planet of Earth, will be in physical form during this new era of awakening, and they will be the teachers; they will be God's shepherds.

Slowly but surely, all will come to pass. And the universal symbol, your six-pointed star that symbolizes the duality expression of mankind—the two unities, one of physical nature and one of spiritual essence—will become the symbol and the power of the Aquarian Age. No longer will they be divided. No longer will the weak, karmic expressions that tend to cause hardships and dissension be present within Earth's frequencies. And the two trinities will become eternally sealed in a united, balanced fashion, for this is the order of things to come.

Incarnated Atlanteans all over your world will be impressed in their minds to relate their energies and their activities to the geometric triangular figures, for these will signify methods of completion for them. It is through the triangles that mankind will project the mind further and further into Atlantean consciousness, and begin to utilize it to greater degrees upon the planet Earth.

*This ends my period of sharing with you on
this occasion. Know that I am with you.
As each day passes, you will become more and
more aware of my presence. You may begin to
draw upon Our vibrations to assist you in all
areas of your needs. I send you the Blessings
of the Universe.*

2

This is Adamis speaking. Bless you.

We speak to you this evening of Universal Law as it pertains to the Atlantean souls. We will see how it applies to them during these present times, through the conflict that has arisen for them in the lower patterns that are part of the planet Earth's progress and evolution.

THE AWAKENING

All those souls who experienced incarnation of service in the vibrations of Atlantis, who are incarnated upon the planet Earth at this time, are undergoing an awakening. Slowly, the doors to these areas are beginning to open for them, and the recall of their activities and their heritage is coming into consciousness. This is, of course, by design, for within the age that your planet has entered, this Age of Enlightenment, it is time for those abilities and talents to once again be expressed and utilized properly by mankind.

There are many side-effects that are taking place with the release of this energy to consciousness. There are many who are experiencing increasingly, uncomfortable feelings within their accustomed normal level of social environment. They are finding themselves involved in detachment, moving away, seeming apart from others. Where do their responsibilities lie? Sadly, there are many who have left their path, many who have chosen to maintain their involvement in the emotional, karmic vibrations of the planet Earth. Of course, this is their choice.

THE UNIVERSAL LAW OF EVOLUTION OF SOUL

Our reason for choosing to share this subject with you is to make it easier for those who have determined that they will continue to walk with God to fulfill their Atlantean heritage once again. We wish to enable them to make this adjustment properly, and with the greatest amount of understanding for themselves. There is a Law of the Universe relating to the evolution of a soul, which states: "When a soul has determined its pattern of truth expression relating to a vibration of experiences, it is no longer subject to the karmic expression that pertains to these experiences." What this means is, for those of you who have endured karmic conditions assigned to Earth elsewhere, and have determined your truth as a result of these past involvements, it is not necessary to allow yourselves to become involved within these energies once again.

You will, of course, be involved with a higher frequency of this same pattern in the future, but at a higher level, not at a lower level. Herein lies the trap for so many of God's children. There are many reasons for falling into this trap. One of these is to avoid being noticed, to avoid feeling different. One accepts and allows oneself to "fit in," so as not to be noticed and stand out alone. Others do not wish to cause problems, or to create conflicts and disagreements. But you must understand that part of your function and your service here is to be an expression of your truth at all times, without any exceptions.

Take yourself back to the days when you were incarnated within the energies of Atlantis. You find that it did not matter who disagreed or agreed with your words and actions and thoughts, for you were aware of your purpose and function, and you followed it to the letter. That is what developed your strength and purpose of mind, and that is what will unite and hold you together during these current days.

It has been said many times that the growth of a soul never steps backwards, that one never truly has to relearn past levels of growth. However, if you accept within your vibrations old patterns of experience once again, you will endure it once again, for you have opened yourself to these energies, and you will find yourself enmeshed in these conflicts once again. This will cause frustration for you.

The modern laws of your society tells you in your marital contract that you are to love one another until death do you part. For you who are subject to Universal Law, it is already your truth that you are to love all, "one another," the same. It is your truth that you are to complete this love within an emotional expression according to your desires, but the true aspect and expression of love must be extended to all in an equal manner. There are none better, none worse. The distinction comes with the application of your emotions. Heed this, My children, for it will spare you much grief and sorrow.

THE UNIVERSAL LAW OF FREE WILL EXPRESSION

There is a Law that states: "When a soul is involved

in an incarnation of voluntary service for God, and in the course of that incarnation does not fulfill the obligations of the contract, the contract itself automatically becomes renewed." What does this mean to you? It could have several interpretations. Let me put your mind at ease, and please remember what we have said to you in the past—that you, as a conscious personality, are not responsible for the actions of your soul, that you as a conscious personality have not existed in the past. You exist for the duration of a single incarnation, and all energy is then absorbed by the soul.

As an example, let us say that you are consciously aware of the service mission of your soul, and you are not in agreement as to placing yourself in this service capacity. It is not something that is to your liking, for you have desires and wants in other areas of expression. When the incarnation will have come to an end, your soul will not have achieved what it came here to achieve. What takes place? What occurs is that the soul will be involved in another expression to accomplish the same task or mission for God. It will not involve you as a conscious mind, for you will not be here. There will be another conscious personality that will be involved in the attempt once more to complete this pattern of service. This is the Universal Law of Free Will Expression.

What I have said to you is not as cut-and-dried as it may seem to be. When a conscious being becomes aware of the existence of it's soul, there is a feeling of oneness that takes place. There is a blending of the Higher and conscious minds into one, sometimes to such a fine degree that there no longer seems to be a separation of the two, and you begin to feel that you and your soul are as one. When the incarnation has expired, the soul has taken with it all of this conscious personality and knowledge, and brings it back once again. Perhaps it will utilize it in the future, perhaps not. But it always retains these past experiences, and has the capacity to bring it forth to consciousness should the occasion arise. A truth is a truth, and when one makes a commitment, the commitment must be fulfilled—if not now, then at some point within the future. But all will be done.

PREPARING YOURSELF FOR THE RISING

Before the year of 1985 comes to a close, all who carry with them the Atlantean vibrations and energies must become aware of their identities. They must have endured the trials of release. They must have rid themselves of all energies and reactions that serve as drains and stumbling blocks to dam up the flow of evolution and energy through their channels.

How is this to be accomplished? I urge you to place yourself in a program of releasing, as part of a weekly pattern of your life. Be involved within the releasing of areas and reactions that are yours and yours alone. Understand that every time you have endured rejection within your current existence, every time you have been victimized by a verbal denial, there has been a reaction in your subconscious mind. There has been implanted there a small degree of unworthiness and lack of compatibility of expression, and all must be released into the care of The Father.

The complexity of what is taking place inside your physical structure is of great magnitude. The crystallization process requires the clearing of ancient constrictions of all blocks of unworthiness in relation to self and to God. If you are, indeed, capable of accepting yourself as a Child of the Universe, then you must, of necessity, accept yourself in an equitable position with the energies of God. You must not place yourself in positions of unworthiness, in positions of fear and awe, for if you do, your energies cannot flow to completion. The most beautiful thing in the world is knowledge, for with knowledge comes sureness of self. With sureness of self also come the energies of a form of isolation, a form of aloneness and separateness. One begins to understand that he is apart from others. But this is in order. This is the way it must be for you, for that is who you are.

Have you ever listened to a friend or acquaintance tell you that he is trying to become a friend to his child, saying that he has spent an entire day sitting and playing in friendship with his child, and that he is pleased. He should not be pleased. A child of three should have friends who are three, not friends who are mature. A child of three does not need its parent to be its friend. It needs a parent to be a parent. It needs the parent to serve the path it has chosen—one of guidance and leadership, of discerning what is right and what is wrong, so that the child may be guided in the proper direction.

Atlantean souls are here as parents. They are not expected to be sisters and brothers to their children. They are expected to be, in a degree, separate—to guide and counsel, to explain. If you have incarnated here in a role you must accept the role. One cannot say to oneself and to others, "I am here to teach, but I shall not present myself in the capacity of a teacher apart from the others. I will sit in their midst and be unnoticed, so I can be as they are." If this occurs, their ears will be closed and they will not hear, for they have come to hear a teacher who is not in attendance. Life, and its expression, is a game. At one moment, one may serve in the capacity of a teacher, and at another in the capacity of a student. Understand that there are all levels of students and teachers, and one cannot be a student of another who has no growth and evolution to offer.

I am not trying to relate these words to you in a soft manner. I am speaking to you in Universal Truth. I am not trying to create a separateness between levels of soul evolution, just of purpose and responsibility. There must be a distinction between the souls that are here involved in that pattern of their growth and those who are here to serve them. The one who is here to serve must stand alone, or his service cannot be accomplished.

Let us look back into history. Let us begin with the expression of Moses, and notice all the trials and turmoil that took place in his efforts to bring the Hebrews to Oneness with God. Look at the periodic rebellions. Look at the periodic denials of God. Look at the Ceasars; look at the Master Jesus; look at Peter and the other disciples. In the end, all suffered. If we ask ourselves, in truth, did they achieve the purposes of their incarnations here, we might come to the conclusion that, after they, in some measure, suffered defeat, others brought it to a successful conclusion.

Did they themselves effect completion, or did they allow themselves to become embroiled within the energies and emotions of others? There is not a Master who has walked the face of the planet Earth who has not expressed an imperfection within his existence, and this will always be. In the beginning, none of them accepted who they were. None of them considered themselves worthy to carry the Star of God. In this unworthiness, to a degree, they involved themselves within the vibrations of mankind, to "fit in"—to be as sisters and brothers, to be as playmates, to be accepted as equals, when this was not their function and not their role.

It is a time for lessons for mankind. The key is to relate to the masses, but not be of them. If the Garden of Eden is to come to pass upon the planet Earth, the Elders must accept their identities, and must accept their worthiness in relation to these identities. They must express themselves and fulfill their service to God. You are who you are, not who you seem to be. The "seem to be" is the facade, the insecurity that you present to the balance of mankind so that you will not suffer rejection and stares and remarks by others.

AN ASSIGNMENT FOR ATLANTEANS

I give you an assignment. I give this assignment to all the Atlanteans who are incarnated upon this planet. Seek out and find one of your sisters and brothers. Find one during the course of each of your months, and wherever you are, bring them within your Circle of Light, to help them understand that they are not walking alone. Tell them that, although they relate to mankind, there is a level to which they belong, something they can be part of.

I cannot stress the importance of this for you. You are in a time of action, and if you have committed yourself to you and to your truth, then this must be an expression of your truth. It is not your work to sit in your circles and share your love with those who already know who you are. You are to share your love with those who have yet to experience it, so that you may expand the sphere of your influence and of your vibrations.

ATLANTEAN LAW

We speak to you now on the subject of Atlantean

Law. We are going to discuss laws pertaining to the different caste levels that existed in Atlantis, and we do so to help you understand and bring them back to your consciousness. This will enable you to realize why you have certain feelings that may seem to be in conflict with certain legal expressions in your current social structure.

Each individual is responsible to himself for the conduct and truthful expression of his life. This includes accountability for actions, and for the results of actions. What does the word "accountability" mean? Does it mean that one must be accountable to another for an action that one takes? This is invalid. One must be accoutable only to self, under the assumption that the action taken was taken in truth. In every civilization in the history of mankind accountability has become a dominant stumbling block to agreements and peace.

The conscious personality of an individual is accountable to itself in truth. Does this mean that the personality is *not* accountable to the soul? Does it mean that the conscious personality is *not* accountable to those with whom it has committed itself? That is correct. No one has a right, in a universal expression, to commit himself of anything to another, only to himself. Think about this statement for a moment. Allow me to pose a question. How can one individual commit himself to another in truth, when truth is constantly in a state of change? The word "commitment" means "agreement under existing conditions." Conditions are never the same; therefore, when one takes an action of committing to another, it cannot be completed in truth. The only commitment that does not change is the soul commitment to God, for that is the only reality that exists. Take the word "commitment" out of your vocabulary; replace it with the word "share," and say to others, "I am pleased to share of myself with you." You will find this more comfortable.

There is an Atlantean Law that states quite simply that all souls are equal. If we expand the meaning of this law, it leaves us to understand that we are not to judge one another, we are not to assume superior or inferior positions in relation to another. We are to acknowledge that, at any given moment, one of us may not consciously be aware of our higher evolution and knowledge. We must look at this from a point-of-view that, if we are aware of our evolution and knowledge, we have been given an opportunity to teach and assist others to grow. It is a tool that we possess. The violation of this Law played an important role in the downfall and destruction of Atlantis, and it certainly has played a dominant role in many of your conflicts upon the surface of Earth.

Within the Plans of God, all souls are equal. When the function of this Universe has been completed, when its role within the vibrations of Creation has been ful-filled, all souls will stand together as One. All will have been completed, and all will be as One. You are aware that whatever is to be is now. Only the conscious know-ing is not present.

If you can apply this within your lives, if you can look at those with whom you are involved in a sharing capacity, and not look at them with frustrations, you will *not* say to others, "I cannot reach this one; he does not seem to be interested in this aspect of his life." If you will do this, you will not feel frustrations or anxieties or pressures upon yourself, for you will then allow every-one to be exactly where they have chosen to be. You will know that the soul is not suffering a loss of growth, that it is evolved, and when all has come to pass, it will be as you. Leave them alone; allow them their own

22

expressions. Do not involve them within your truth unless it is asked of you. Acknowledge that others have different needs during their current expression of truth.

CREATING ONENESS

If mankind is to create one world, it can be one world only in relation to the freedom of expression and choice. It cannot be one world where all beings are consciously aware to the same degree, for then there would be no learning experiences. We need to have souls striving for the oneness, the acceptance, the allowance leading to the commitment to oneself and to God. It is within this universal capacity of existence that all of the Atlanteans everywhere must come together. They must come to the realization of these identities so that they can be of service to the balance of mankind. They are not to be aloof, only to understand and accept their roles.

ADULTERY

Do not be an Atlantean who is committing adultery. We discuss this word with you within the context of your Atlantean knowledge. If I could laugh, I would. If one of your dictionaries were present during ancient days, the definition and completeness of this word "adultery" would be "unfaithfulness to oneself." That is the total, true spiritual meaning of this word, and it bears no relationship to another human being. If one is committing adultery to oneself, one is also committing adultery to God. We are committing adultery when we deny the existence of God without, as well as the God within. We are committing adultery when we allow ourselves to be pushed and steered into actions to keep peace, when we know they are not our truths.

If this be the case, then how did mankind finally resolve itself into other definitions for this word? Where did mankind go wrong? Perhaps a long time ago, within ancient histories upon earth, a marital contract signified a possession, and it was said, "If you impose yourself upon my possession, you are committing adultery." But how can this apply to the Child of the Universe who is aware that the only thing one possesses is self, and the only way one can adulterate himself is to himself, for that is all he has. One who accusses another of adultery is living in an expression of self-lies, for he deceives himself into owning and possessing. All that has occurred is an action.

If I share my truth with you, and your response to my truth is denial and accusations and jeers, I could say to you, "You are committing adultery upon my truth." You are raping my energies. That is not valid, for you cannot rape my energies; only I can do that. If I stand in anger, and be the cause of the undesirable result of an action, and raise a fist to God, I am committing adultery, for I know my truth, and I am denying it. All adultery involves yourself in an action that you are aware denies your truth.

Bring yourselves together in your minds and your hearts. Examine the nooks and crannies of your expressions; search your soul; invest your time and your efforts in these areas, for the benefits that will result to you are ones that will be of great peace and growth.

STRIVING FOR FULL DIMENSIONS

In your meditations, close your eyes and bring the six-pointed universal star into your perception. Notice that it is one-dimensional, flat, without depth, without perceptibility. Begin to expand its dimensions. Create in your mind one behind another, and another, and another, to add solidarity and depth within this structure. Create the expansion of your awareness. Travel with your mind into the depths of the six triangulations of the corners, and find where they take you.

You have discovered, over years, that the planet Earth is not flat, that it has depth and dimensions and character, and so does your Universe. Create the depths of your own private universe, and begin to explore them, and in the exploration you will begin to become comfortable with your identity as Children of your Universe.

The key to the success of Atlantis was the conscious knowledge of identity of soul. This acceptance afforded all the opportunity to open the conscious mind without restrictions to soul knowledge and abilities. This must come to pass in your Aquarian Age, for there are many things that await mankind.

Blessings.

3

This is Adamis.

In order to serve in the proper capacity for completing the understandings of ancient Atlantean frequencies and functions, it is necessary for individuals at this present time to be aware of the causative patterns of karmic energy that are affecting their lives.

THE TRIANGLE OF FREQUENCIES OF THE AQUARIAN AGE

It has been said that the triangle of frequencies that compose your Aquarian Age consist of the frequencies of Atlantis, of Moses and the Twelve Tribes of Israel, and of the energies of those who walked with the Master Jesus. All Atlantean souls that walked upon the planet Earth during those eras of Earth's history are, indeed, physically incarnated upon the Earth plane at this present time.

In order to have the whole, we must have the sum of the total of the parts. That is why they are present here. In their presence upon the Earth plane, they have brought with them the frequencies and knowledge of their Atlantean expressions. For many years, much of this knowledge has laid dormant in their unconscious minds. The evolution of the planet Earth's vibrations has stimulated the sleeping frequencies and begun to cause them to pour forth at the conscious level.

We will discuss the results of this outpouring of energy and recollection of expression. It would be an untruth to say to you that, because of the level of soul involved within the Elder expression of Atlantis, the Elders were beyond creating karmic conditions for themselves, for this certainly was not the truth. Always be advised that, whenever a soul incarnates and confines itself in a physical structure involved with emotional and free-will expression, at least two choices always present themselves. This, of course, was the case for many of the souls incarnating as Elders in Atlantis.

As the minds of those who were the Elders continually open to their ancient heritage, they are slowly becoming aware of deeds of imperfection that their conscious expressions committed during the Atlantean era. Many have emotionally taken upon themselves expressions of guilt, sadness, and remorse, in relation to these deeds. Some of these actions have been consciously related through the presence of psychics and mediums, and this has caused great emotional distress. It is now time for us to establish the Divine Truth in relation to this period of history, and in relation to soul involvement within the karmic experience.

THE DIVINE TRUTH

Try to accept these words: All actions taken by conscious personalities in any physical expression do not necessitate or require the adopting of this karmic condition by future conscious personalities. With each incarnation, the soul acquires a new personality and subconscious expression; therefore, it is not in order, in the highest sense of the word, for a new personality to assume guilt and responsibility for conditions another personality has taken unto itself. I say to you from the highest order of truth, it is not proper, under any conditions, for a conscious individual ever to invoke the energies of guilt or remorse in relation to action assumed in a past life expression. This statement is irrevocable and without exception.

The proper course of attitude is for one, upon becoming aware of this prior experience or situation, to volunteer to assist the soul in the conscious alleviation of these energy aberrations, to assist in joy and blessings rather than to hang the head in shame and remorse, to take the actions in the opposite expression to totally alleviate these conditions. Always have your cup of truth and joy overflowing. Never allow the energies of joy to seep out of the bottom of the glass. Let them overflow.

RESPONSIBILITIES OF ATLANTEAN SOULS

It is the obligation of all Atlantean souls in the Age of Aquarius to transmit to conscious personalities the knowledge and experience of all things that occurred during the ancient civilization. The purpose for this is not to punish nor to create guilt, but to educate. In the education, the personality will become aware of the steps and attitudes it must avoid during the present experience. Only in this manner can these energies be relieved. Only in this manner will the conscious personality be able, at least, to fulfill the purpose for the ancient Elders coming to Earth. As time passes, the con-

29

scious mind will be impressed in more rapid order with the awareness of responsibility for the New Age.

The awakening and accepting of the responsibility will weigh heaily upon the shoulders of those who come into this consciousness. For this reason, it is most important to begin to seek out those who are as yourselves. If there is one fact and one attitude that you must always carry in the forefront of your thoughts, it is the one pertaining to your heritage and to your true Universal identity. This will enable you to be constantly on the alert to receive frequencies from others that are compatible with your own, causing you a recognition, one to the other, of a sister or brother in the highest order of Truth.

The Atlantean souls are here as God's shepherds. You are here to return the flocks to the Lord. This cannot be accomplished without acceptance of your own identity, without release of ancient, unwarranted guilt, and certainly without putting aside the weight of karmic responsibility.

The Elders are upon the planet Earth in service for mankind. In the highest order, it is their prerogative to release all frequencies of energy that are deemed to be obstacles toward this achievement. If they have the strength, if they have the belief and the willingness to serve, it is within the realm of their power to release their involvement in all karmic frequencies associated with the planet Earth. Upon the desire and the statement of release, all will dissipate, and the personality will, from that moment forth, be free to serve unobstructed in a clear manner.

One might ask, "How can this be in order?" The answer is quite simple. If the conscious mind can bring itself to the point of acknowledging its soul as a Child of the Universe, here on the planet Earth to serve, it can be done. The mere statement relieving oneself of karmic responsibility relating to the lower Earth's frequencies acknowledges the validity of one's detachment from these energies, and consequently enables one from that moment to begin to serve in truth.

We are now going to share with you utilizing the knowledge and frequencies of one who walked upon your planet Earth under the vibrations of Pythagoras.

These are the energies of Pythagoras.

GEOMETRIC TRIANGULATIONS

The ancient Atlanteans utilized in a conscious manner the universal truth of geometric triangulations to the highest degree of efficiency. At the same time, they utilized these geometrics ultimately to cause their downfall and destruction. This must be avoided at all costs in the future, and it is to this end that we bring you the following information for your understanding.

As with all universes, your Universe is composed of four quadrants of Creative Mass Light. Each subsequent division of your Universe—galaxies, solar systems, planets themselves—are within the geometric influence of these quadrants. Each quadrant is a triangulation of energy that influences one-quarter of your Earth's population, and is the fundamental energy expression of purpose and evolution for these souls.

THE THREE-DIMENSIONAL SIX-POINTED STAR

When the Planet of Atlantis was destroyed and the souls reincarnated upon the surface of Earth, they brought with them their knowledge pertaining to the universal geometric triangulations. When the Hierarchy of the Universe had determined the six basic karmic frequencies to be involved within mankind's expression and evolution, two triangulations were created and inherently blended together into what you refer to as your six-pointed star.

Your comprehension and understanding of the integration of these vibrations has, during your Piscean Era, been confined to a one-dimensional representation of these energies. As your minds expand and you become aware of the multi-dimensional expression of knowledge contained within your soul, it is necessary for you to begin to relate to the energies within this universal geometrics in three-dimensional expression and manifestation. To this end, we have transmitted the knowledge and method of physically constructing the three-dimensional six-pointed star for you to utilize in your exploration of universal frequencies and dimensions.

To begin to allow your minds the conscious assimilation of these three-dimensional frequencies or the perception of interdimensional knowledge, suspend this device approximately twelve inches over your head, and expose yourself to the interdimensional reaction of energies. This treatment should be for a duration of fifteen of your minutes in length. We strongly advise no more than one exposure to these energies on a daily basis. When your period of exposure has been completed, place yourself in a meditative state, and record the thoughts and impressions and truths that come to your consciousness.

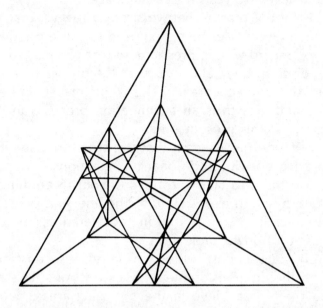

The following will occur to you: All perceptions of truth that you have been emotionally aware of will gradually begin to alter. In the past, your growth has been governed by the spiralling evolution of frequencies. You have been exposed to, and have accepted, definitions of truth expressions. As your evolution has continued, a new interpretation for this expression has come into your mind; and as you have evolved, higher and higher forms of understanding of the same perception have gradually come into your consciousness.

Now the awareness and comprehension will come to you in an interdimensional level instantaneously. I must caution you that the perception and acceptance of interdimensional truth within a short period of time can weigh heavily upon your emotional expressions and associations. It is like making one aware of the constant contents of a complete volume of knowledge, without having to read it page by page.

It is for this reason that we strongly suggest that, in your meditation after being exposed to these frequencies, you record your impressions so that you may study them, discern them, allow yourself the proper time for acclimation and acceptance. This whole measure of exposure and growth is an acceleration process, and is necessary at this present time.

Notice on the diagram that the structure itself has been encased with additional triangulations. The purpose for this is to take you beyond your three dimensions, to begin to expose you to the energy process of communication, transportation, acceleration, by the process of thought projection.

Your souls, in past expressions in Atlantis, consciously used multidimensional energy expressions. This enabled them to achieve in the following areas: dematerialization—direct conscious mental communication with divisions of the Space Commands—conscious awareness of the source of their quadrant energy existence—the ability for the soul to leave the physical structure when service in an incarnation had been completed, and direct alignment with ultra-rays of universal energy for use in healing and spiritual communication. These are the ultimate results that we desire you to achieve through exposure to this multidimensional six-pointed star.

AREAS FOR DEVELOPMENT

We are going to prescribe a list of subjects for you to be concerned with in relation to your development and evolution into Universal Truth. These areas involve your emotional as well as spiritual reactions and understandings. The procedure is as follows:

Set the condition in your mind to be made aware of Universal Truth relating to, for example, recognition of God-Self. Sit and experience the multidimensional actions and energies that result. Record your feelings, record your emotional reactions.

We strongly urge you not to involve yourself in this process concerning more than one specific area at a time. Occasionally, each area will involve more than one session. Complete one area. Allow it to be in total acceptance and understanding before proceeding to the next.

The areas of involvement are as follows:

1. Knowledge of God-Self
2. Assimilation with Soul called Universal God
3. Vibrations of the following expressions:
   A. Love
   B. Truth
   C. Commitment
   D. Acceptance
   E. Detachment
   F. Sin
   G. Karma
   H. Guilt
   I. Adultery
   J. Carnal Expression
   K. Union with Others
   L. Flow of Substance
   M. Worthiness
   N. Acceptance of Purpose for Incarnation

In addition to the above-mentioned, allow the energies to be experienced one at a time through each of the basic seven chakras in the body.

As you can see, there is much work ahead for you. The proper placement and acceptance in these areas of your expression will take you a considerable amount of time and effort. You must decide if you are willing to devote the effort and the time into this project to achieve the desired results. In your search to bring your heritage into consciousness, if you are compatible with what you believe to be your purpose and truth here relating to your service, this will be the incentive for you to pursue this avenue of evolution.

Your soul is already aware of all that we have just mentioned to you. Now it is time for your conscious personality to align itself totally with the knowledge and divine truth of your soul. Only in this manner can you truly express yourself in your Atlantean consciousness and serve as a shepherd for God.

We reiterate, in each step of this program, it is of the utmost importance for you to continually express your feelings and emotions in the expression of writing, to enable you to release and to experience all that is occurring to you so that you can adequately face the changes and expressions you are enduring. Find one with whom you are vibrationally attuned. The two of you share this process together in truth so that each of you will have a support system, someone to lean upon through the course of this process.

We now withdraw these energies. They will share again in the continuing expression of this volume of knowledge.

This is Kryon speaking.

THE GOLDEN TRIAD

If you will arrange to expose yourself to a color of light of soft but strong gold frequency during the same time that you are involved within the energies of the three-dimensional six-pointed star, it will magnetically assist you in the completion and experiencing of these frequencies. You may do this through use of an external physical light source, or mentally by bathing yourself in the energies of the Golden Triad. Either method will be quite satisfactory for you.

When the original triangulation of great "fire" crystals was set into place in the reconstruction of Atlantis, the vibrations of the Golden Triad were the energies utilized to complete this interaction of magnetics. From these frequencies were drawn off the assimilative frequencies to enable the Elders to convert energy into matter, to convert thought into reality, to transport mind and structure wherever desired.

When the time is proper and your vibrations are in accord, you will be branded symbolically with the sign of the Triad upon your brow. This will be your medallion of truth and of completion. Some of you will be instructed to wear a mediallion of the Triad physically around your neck, as a protection and completion of your frequencies. This amulet will be used as a healing instrument, as a mind projection frequency for yourself as well as for application to others. Those who wear the medallion will assume universal responsibility for incarnated beings within the same quadrant of soul expression.

Before the medallion is set into place in a symbolic fashion, all of the conditioning stated to you by the energies of Pythagoras must be in proper order and vibrational frequency. This is necessitated by the fact that, in the total expression of service, one must have elevated himself above involvement with the karmic vibrations that have been assigned to the planet Earth. This detachment must be total, for one cannot ever be allowed to express, in any manner, primarily from an emotional reaction. All expressions must be instigated from the level of mind, and the emotions should be utilized as the completion factor of the mind expression. Do not consider that this will cause you to be a "cold person," for this will not be. All it will do for you is to enable you to be totally in control, expressing yourself in truth at all times.

Now we return the frequency channel to Adamis.

Before you commence with the exercises described by Pythagoras, it is advisable for you to place yourself in meditation, totally confirming and becoming comfortable with your Atlantean heritage. Call upon God to bring you the strength that you may accept yourself. If you have felt or known that you are here to serve mankind, do not concern yourself with ego expression relating to this acceptance. Acknowledge your identity, acknowledge your purpose, and set out upon your path of fulfillment. There are many to support you, many for you to share with, many for you to achieve the fulfillment of expression with.

Blessings.

4

This is "Strength" from Atlantis. Greetings.

THE ATLANTEAN CHANTS

Among the ancient vibrations of the civilization of Atlantis were frequencies that were chanted in tones. These have been shared with you and have been designated as the "Atlantean Chants." The resonance of these sounds served the Atlanteans and are here to serve you in stimulating the frequencies of your meridians to assist you in the fulfillment of many of your endeavors. This pertains to healing, to recall at the conscious level, as well as to aspects of space and spiritual communication.

The relationship to the universal interlocking triangles of six points is fundamental for use in conjunction with color frequency and magnetics. This is the ultimate expression of the blending of energies of Truth and Order to effect healing polarity frequencies, as well as the energies of regeneration. The resonant sounds are universal. The color frequencies are ultra-frequencies, also of universal origin. We are going to describe for you the process of healing with sound, color, and crystals.

#1: A-LE-U   #2: BA-O

These chants are used to prepare the individual's vibrations for meditation and for learning. They unblock energy and allow for the flows of information and for peace to commence. They place the balance of energies in your meridians in order. They place the opening of your chakras in unison, for under normal conditions some of your chakras will be more open than others. These chants create harmony and equal amplification distributed within the seven basic chakras. Before chanting, bring the twenty-seventh ultra-ray of Light, the ray of silvery pink, into your presence. Lie down, place seven single-terminated crystals, all pointed toward your head, one on each chakra, and chant three times.

#3:   GA-MO-AL

This is utilized for diseases relating to the liver, the pancreas, the spleen, and the kidneys. The chant is used in conjunction with the seventeenth ray of persimmon, banded in silver. The ray is inserted and applied through a spiritual chakra located five inches above the small of the back on the spine. Set the person in a pattern of clusters on copper wire. Use two clusters on each side, in line with the navel, the point of the triangulation, and place two clusters between the knees.

#4: DOU-LAE   #6: VO-A-A

These chants apply to the variable frequencies of energy connected with the respiratory system. It is associated with the sixteenth ray of lemon-pink, banded on each side in gold. Place a triangulation of crystals on the upper half of the body—one on each shoulder with the points downward, and one on the navel with the point upward. You may also set a pattern of double clusters on copper wire—one along each shoulder, with the point placement between the legs, approximately at mid-thighs.

#5: HA-JO-HA

This is the resonance to call upon God's Light to heal with the powers of regeneration. It is associated with the twenty-second ray of pearlized White Light, banded in gold. Mentally activate the crystal implantations in the palms of your hands that are emerald green in color. While you are chanting and have the twenty-second ray in your mind, complete the healing, as the energy in a trinity of frequency flows through your hands to the subject.

#7: ZOO-UR   #8: CHO-RA*

These chants are utilized in association with past-life regression and experiences. Call upon the nineteenth ray of pale green and gold, banded in silver, to assist you. Place single-terminated crystals in the following places on the body: one over your spiritual eye, point downward; one on your heart chakra in the center of your chest, point upward; and one in the palm of each hand, with the points toward your shoulders. As you chant and experience the ray of pale green and gold, the energies that are dormant relating to your past-life experiences and abilities will slowly come into your conscious mind.

#9: TU-LA-RO

This is utilized for all conditions of arthritis, nerve inflammation, and skin eruptions. It is associated with

---

*See also Chant #19.

the color of pale rose. Place the subject, or yourself, in a pattern of twelve single-terminated crystals, or use the double-diamond pattern of cluster crystals. If the disease is of advanced nature, you will find the pattern of clusters will be more effective than the single-terminated crystals.

#10:   YO-OOH-DA

These are the sounds of the God Within. It is to be chanted in conjunction with the thirty-sixth ray of Light, the perception of all color. When you are ready to acknowledge the total existence of God, and are ready to reach beyond into the Creative Mass, use this to assist you in your expansion. Place yourself in a pattern of twelve single-terminated crystals. Set a triangle overlay on your body: one on the third eye, one on the throat, and one on the heart chakra, all pointing toward the top of your head. Please note that, even though these crystals are physically in a straight line, spiritually they form an energy triangle for you.

#11:   CO-LAE-AH

This relates to the healing of physical deformities, broken bones after they have been set, and healing after surgery. The chant is used in association with the color red. This assignment has been made because these frequencies are mainly physical Earth vibrations used in conjunction with the energies of the nature spirits. Set a pattern of three single-terminated crystals over the area involved. The pattern can be either in a physical straight line for healing of arms and legs or in triangulation for areas of the torso. Whichever pattern is utilized, place all the points facing toward the Earth or, if the subject is lying down, toward your feet.

#12: LAU-RR-U   #2: BA-O

These chants are associated with diseases pertaining to the lower extremities that result from circulatory problems and muscular disorders. We utilize the twenty-first ray of orange-yellow, banded in silver. Place single-terminated crystals on the chakras at the top of each hip, and one on the ball of each of your feet. The crystals at the hips points downward, the ones on the balls of the feet point upward. You may also use a triangle of double clusters: the base at the waist, and the point slightly past the bottom of your feet. The clusters must be placed upon a triangle of copper wire.

#13:   MO-RAA-AH

This is used to achieve a balance between the male and female vibrational expressions. It is used in conjunction with the twentieth ultra-ray of lilac and lavender, banded in gold. This is particularly effective in dealing with problems of sexual self-acceptance and worthiness. Place a single-terminated crystal on the following areas: one on the base chakra, pointing upward, one on the throat chakra, pointing downward; and one on the heart chakra, pointing upward. This pattern will assist you in opening blocks relating to your own emotional and sexual self-acceptance and awareness. Understand that what is to be achieved here bears no relationship to any involvement between yourself and another individual. This exercise is purely between you and your own experiences of worthiness.

#14: NO-OH-RAH   #15: SO-MAA-AH

These are Universal vibrations of self-acceptance relating to ego and soul. It is used with the frequencies of deep purple for strength, to gain incentives for spiritual achievement. Hold single-terminated crystals in the palm of each of your hands with the points upward. Place one crystal on your heart center with the point upward to complete the pattern.

#16: O-OH-DA   #17: FAA-RO

These resonances align you with the frequences of the nature spirits. It is utilized with the thirty-third ultra-ray of palest rose. In a sitting poisition, hold a single-terminated crystal in each hand with the point touching the ground. As you are chanting, it will bring your energies into harmony and call forth recognition of the energies of Earth and of the nature spirits. Within a reasonable period of time, communication will be achieved for you in this area of spiritual compatibilities.

#18:   ZAU-RAAM

This is an intense, resonating sound. It is used in conjunction with the energies of emerald green, associated with Luke, the Master of the Healing Frequencies for the planet Earth. Mentally activate the etheric crystal implantation circuitry in your body. As you are chanting, this will stimulate your energies, particularly your healing frequencies in preparation for healing applications. This is to be used as a preparatory amplification for you when you are to involve yourself in any healing practice or procedure. It also can be used as a protective device for yourself when you are going to be exposed to any sort of negative energy. This would apply when one is going to visit someone in a hospital or when one works in a counseling capacity and is exposed to negativity all of the time. It creates, in essence, a force field of healing vibrations that can tend to seal you away from invasion of negative frequencies of energy.

#19: KO-FAA-ROO   #8: CHO-RA

Use these chants in relation to working with children. We use it in conjunction with the eighteenth ray of soft, pale, French blue, banded in gold. Place the child in a pattern of the six-pointed star. When you have invoked the ray, place the child in the pattern and chant the resonance. This energy bypasses the personality and opens the child's soul to your mind. It helps you become aware of the soul's purpose for the physical involvement with this condition. This system is particularly effective when dealing with children who have karmic expressions such as mental retardation, Down's Syndrome, and autism, for it enables one to reach the soul, and through communications to learn what can be done to assist in achieving what the soul is here to achieve.

#20:   RU-AH-SHIM

A chant to heal utilizing magnetics. Its function is to unify the etheric crystallization process. In addition, by invoking the twenty-fifth ray of lemon-yellow, it opens you to communication with the energies of the Space Brotherhoods, as well as the frequencies of Solomon. Sit at a table. Erect a triangle of six single crystals, the point of the triangle coming to you, the base of the triangle further away from you. All the crystals point toward you. When the triangle has been completed, lay three more single crystals in a straight line from the point toward you again. This pattern of nine will amplify and concentrate the energies as they are channeled to you.

#21: SHE-MA

When chanted with the thirty-fourth ray, the palest of violets, this brings you into alignment with the energies known as Sananda, the feminine aspect of God. These are the vibrations of Love, Softness, and Unity. Sit in a triangle of single-terminated crystals, with the apex behind you and all crystals pointing toward the back. Chant it to a loved one, and it will bring your frequencies into harmony. Chant it to yourself, and chant it to God as well.

#22: TRI-AAH

This is chanted in association with the color of soft pastel rose. Place a single-terminated crystal on the shoulder with the point downward, one in the palm of the hand with the point upward, and one at the junction of the elbow, pointed in either direction. This process is to be utilized for all conditions existing in the shoulders and arms, such as bursitis, arthritis, and nervous disorders. It may be used on both sides simultaneously.

#23: THU-MAAR

Chant these frequencies in conjunction with the twenty-eighth ray. These are three alternating stripes of powder blue with two of gold--five stripes in all. Use the extended crystal pattern as described in #20, the one involving the nine crystals. This will assist you in receiving Universal frequencies and communication.

#24: AU-MA-LAA

This final chant is a resonance to protect you from outside "invasion" of your energies, as well as from negativity. It is used with the thirtieth ray of the palest of orange. Keep your "personal" crystal with you at all times. When utilizing this trinity of energies, place the crystal over your heart, and then chant. This places a shield around you to protect your energies. This is to be used more as a protection from spiritual invasion than from acquiring negativity from an emotional level.

PERSONAL FREQUENCIES OF ENERGY

In time to come, your scientists and health practitioners will evolve a process by which a single frequency of energy will be disseminated to an individual. This frequency of energy will be a combination of the resonance, the color, and the magnetics associated with a specific organ in the physical structure. The exposure to this single frequency of light will instantaneously regenerate the organ to perfection.

However, as long as mankind is involved within carnal, karmic vibrations, this will not come to pass. The planet Earth is in the Age of Aquarius. New races of beings, new levels of souls are incarnating upon your planet. In time, the lower bands of karmic frequency will be removed and replaced with ones of more universal relationships. All of the emotional, carnal expressions will have disappeared from the reactive systems of mankind. When this has come to pass, the energies of regeneration will be widely utilized by mankind.

For now, it is in order for your to utilize this trinity of frequencies as we have described. You will find them most effective in your applications. Each time you utilize one of these chants, you will find a greater and greater confirmation for yourself pertaining to your identity, and you realize that you have utilized these resonances in the past.

OTHER FORMS OF COMMUNICATION TO COME

As time passes, additional geometric structures, part of the representation of other methods of communication, will be made available to mankind.* The purity of transmission of magnetics from those involved within the Space Commands will be consciously disseminated to mankind. The communication will appear in the form of rigid and fluid geometric symbols. The purpose for this is to prevent emotional distortion upon receiving the transmission.

Many of these geometric figures will be associated with different color frequencies in your spectrum. The placing of certain colored figures in patterns will begin to generate flows of energy that will have healing effects upon the mind and upon the emotions. You will be instructed as to the proper functions for each of the figures. It will be possible to construct representations of these figures out of copper rods, using colored glass or plastic inserts as required. These figures can then be passed over the body by another to produce the desired geometric frequencies and results.

GEOMETRIC COMMUNICATION

We will now describe the physical representation of geometric communication with the members of the Space Commands. These figures can be physically constructed from heavy rigid copper wire. All of them should have a handle for you to hold in your applications. The inside spaces are to be filled with colored plastic or glass.**

---

*See also Chapter 11.
**See footnote on page 66.

These geometrics are magnetic healing devices that are actually used aboard ships for specific corrective measures. In all applications, the subject should be lying down, in a prone position. Holding the energy paddle by the handle, move it slowly over the entire physical body in slow circles. You may move it in a clockwise or counterclockwise direction. The treatment with each paddle should be in the area of five minutes. It is in order for you to use combinations of paddles. You may hold one in each hand at the same time, or use them consecutively, one after the other.

The paddles do not have to be larger than six by eight inches in overall dimensions, without the handles.

1. Emerald Green

Insert material of the color green in this paddle. It is to be used for the healing of emotional frequencies.

2. Pastel Rose or Pink

This paddle will be colored in pastel rose or pink. Its energies cleanse the auric field and balance the meridian flows on both sides of the body.

3. Deep Blue

The insets will be in the color of deep blue. The function is to harmonize and attune the mind truth with the body truth and the expressive truth.

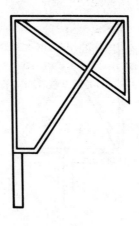

4. Soft Yellow

This paddle is colored in soft yellow. The overall movement of this in relation to the body has the result of giving the mind clarity of knowledge and discernment for the acceptance of educational energies.

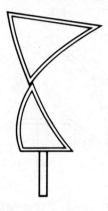

5. Red

The insets will be in the color red. This movement is designed for physical balance, vitality, and structure health. It also aids in breaking down unwanted deposits of fatty tissue, cholesterol, and alkaline or acidic conditions.

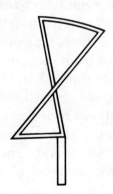

6. Deep Violet

This paddle is colored in deep violet. The prime function for these energies is for removing negative energies from the aura and the physical structure. It is particularly effective in weakening a spiritual possession, enabling it to be removed.

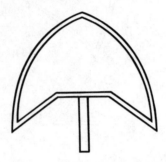

As time passes and it is seen that what we have released to you has been properly utilized for mankind, more will be made available to you.

The science of Universal magnetics and its applications in the expansion of civilizations on Earth is still in its infancy. The blending of spiritual evolvement and greater usage of brain capacity through science will hold the keys for galactic exploration and beyond.

Man, for the most part, conducts his life in relation to what he sees and feels. Your societies have been oriented to base their truths on pure science and physical manifestations. In time, all of this must change. As man grows and evolves, he will begin to understand the temporary condition of his physical realities, such as his body. This spiritual evolution will bring him to the point where he will become more accepting of his soul and all intangibles pertaining to his eternal existence.

5

This is Adamis.

SEED CRYSTALS

Untold eons ago, when it had been determined that the planet Earth was to house Children of Light, magnetics in the form of physical matter were introduced to Earth in order to assist them.

These magnetics took the form of what we refer to as "seed crystals." These crystals were planted—or "seeded"—on Earth by the Space Brothers, exactly as we find them today. They were strategically placed in specific locations, so that the resulting triangulations would generate force fields to lead to the mines and pockets of crystals that you find on Earth at this time.

The crystals are found in two consistent shapes:

Triangular Prism

The first is a balanced triangular prism. It generally measures four to seven inches in length, with a center diameter of one inch. It contains a color frequency that appears as pale amythest.

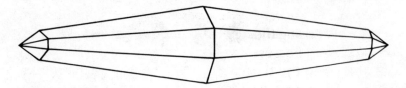

Spire Prism

The second prism has its widest diameter located near the base. It measures six to ten inches in length, and is without color frequency.

Both representations of the seed crystals are in perfect symmetry. To be properly functional, they must not be damaged, and must be double-terminated. They contain the normal six sides and six facets on the top and the bottom.

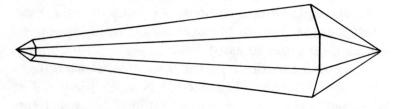

USES OF SEED CRYSTALS

The energies present in the seed crystals are manifested through different frequencies, and are utilized for specific purposes and functions. They are not to be placed in healing patterns, nor are they to be used for healing of isolated physical disease.

When you hold a seed crystal in your hand, you will experience different frequencies of energy from those you normally experience in the handling of quartz crystals. These crystals contain a blending of magnetic frequencies and the regenerative energies of God. They are to be used as instruments of mental, physical, emotional, and spiritual transformation.

Because of the great power of these crystals and their ability to transmute energies, great care must be taken in chosing those who come into their possession. If you are to possess one, know that it will be tendered to you when the time is proper. Do not seek them out. If they have not come to you, it is not time for you to use this instrument. (One might say that this is another lesson for you in the energies of patience.)

The seed crystals were utilized in Atlantis as "control" instruments. An individual, who was to be the subject, would lie down. The balance of the group would place themselves in the same position. The leader would hold the "seed" crystal in one hand, with the narrowest termination gently touching the physical body of the subject, and move it in the desired pattern and direction.

When the mind conditions had been established for the crystal to serve in a control capacity, all others in the room experienced the bodily energy movements to the same intensity and degree as the control subject.

This is important for you to remember. In the future, occasions will arise when groups of people will need healings for the same disruptive conditions. All can be healed through the application of energy to one individual.

The seed crystals were utilized to achieve total alignment of the chakra centers in the physical structure. The narrower termination was placed over the crown chakra and gently moved down the body to the base chakra. All chakras achieved harmonious balance of position as well as compatible frequency of functional energies.

If energy blockages occur in the spine, arm, or leg, the movement of the seed crystal from one energy insertion point to the other will alleviate the blockage and allow the energies to flow in a normal manner.

If you wish to use the seed crystal for self-healing, lie down and hold it in both hands with the narrow termination touching your heart chakra. The ensuing flow of energies will balance your energy meridians and revitalize your physical, mental, and spiritual processes.

EMOTIONAL AND SPIRITUAL BLOCKAGES

The most powerful service the seed crystals perform for mankind relates to the emotional and spiritual blockages that are present in the lives of individuals.

This applies to incarnated souls here in the capacity of Star-Children, Walk-Ins, Atlantean expressions, and Alien service. Due to the nature of their sensitivities, the majority of them experience the following conditions:

1. As children, they discover that their emotional reactions to people and situations are ones of quiet, inner expression.

2. They are uncomfortable having overt expressions of elation and joy, but they try to have them, and thereby cause discomfort and insecurity within themselves.

3. Doubts arise as to their ability to express emotions, and they shield themselves from others to avoid emotional confrontation. Self-unworthiness begins to set in.

4. Their sensual responses are different from others.

5. They always strive to be totally in control of self, and rarely allow themselves a total emotional and sensual expression.

The resulting patterns of expression cause blockages of self-unworthiness emotionally and sexually. These conditions must be relieved before the individuals can move forward into their full pattern of service for God.

SIMILAR BLOCKAGES IN ATLANTIS

These conditions arose in Atlantis. Often, when unions were dissolved, one of the parties became distraught over the dissolution. He emotionally blamed himself and his inadequacies for the dissolution. When this occurred, the individual was placed in a relaxed, meditative position and told to concentrate on his physical heart. Breathing was conducted through the mouth, as the procedure involved physical movement and reactions.

The purpose for this procedure was to release blocked emotions of self-worthiness in the heart, and to allow the individual to experience his self-worth emotionally and sexually.

A seed crystal was placed over the physical heart with the narrower termination gently touching the body. A strand of self-emotion was attached to the crystal and pulled out of the heart and down the physical body. As the person exhaled, he forced the energy down, experiencing the release of the freedom of his emotions.

The strand of Light was then anchored in the base chakra. This, in effect, united the heart and emotions with the sensual, expressive center-of-self.

This process was repeated seven times. Each time, the connection became stronger and stronger. The person breathed heavier and pushed down harder as the connection became stronger. (The physical expression is the same as a woman in child birth.) At the culmination of this process, the individual experienced a total emotional release, and peaceful self-acceptance came to pass.

ACCEPTANCE OF SELF

Upon your planet Earth, during your Age of Aquarius, the proper alignment of your energies and acceptance of self in all areas is of great importance. As time passes and the lower karmic frequencies of emotional experiences are removed from the Earth's energies, you must be in order.

Those who are not in order cannot serve. They will hang on to vestigial vibrations that will lead only to their destruction. The full expression of emotional and physical love must be expressed at a higher frequency of truth and understanding.

THE PHYSICAL STRUCTURE AS A TOOL OF THE SOUL

Many of the ancient Atlanteans did not evolve to this degree. This factor was partly responsible for the destruction of their civilization. They used their physical bodies as primary tools for expression, instead of their minds. They allowed the lower chakras to create conditions that affected others in a carnal, unspiritual manner. This created havoc in the balance of body and mind expressions of energy.

Mankind must understand and accept the presence of the physical structure as an expressive tool of the soul. Its prime purpose is to be a vehicle through which the soul achieves its growth and service. All physical structures serve the same purpose. They merely appear to be different, according to the varying emotional reactions.

Cast aside the shame for your physical structure. Place it in its proper perspective in your truth, and utilize it as a vehicle for the spiritual fulfillment of your soul.

This is Kryon from the Universe Quadrille V speaking.

I am here to describe additional applications for the seed crystals by mankind on the planet Earth.

ADDITIONAL APPLICATIONS FOR SEED CRYSTALS

As time passes, the ability to communicate with spirit and other sources of existence will become increasingly important. The following exercises will enable mankind to achieve this evolution:

Antenna for Universal Energies

The seed crystal is to be used as an "antenna" for universal magnetic energies. Hold it in one hand with the widest termination toward your body. Touch it to your crown chakra for a period of five of your minutes. Follow this procedure at your spiritual third eye, the throat chakra, and the heart chakra. Allow five minutes rest between each application.

The result will be the transmuting of your channeling frequencies into harmony with the universal grid system of communication. This will enable you consciously to achieve this awareness and experience, and to serve others to a greater degree.

Expectant Mothers

During Atlantean times, expectant mothers used seed crystals to assist them consciously in receiving the vibrations of the souls of their unborn children. Now, in your Aquarian Age, souls of Master vibrations are incarnating in multitudes, and it is increasingly important for expectant parents to be aware of the soul's purpose, desired environment, diet, etc. Both parents should be involved in this process.

Place the seed crystal on the woman's stomach, narrow point up. Holding it in both hands, set the condition that the crystal will serve as a connecting link between vibrations, and awareness will come to pass.

Clearing Other Crystals

The seed crystals may be used to clear your other crystals of negative frequencies or of color implantations that you have used previously.

Setting the conditions in your mind, pass the seed crystal over the length of the other crystal three times. This will restore it to total harmony and clarity of energies. Whenever you implant color in a crystal for application, it can be easily removed by following this process.

Location Devices

The seed crystals may also be used as location devices for specific minerals, etc., that are located beneath the surface of the Earth. Hold it in your hand, narrow point down, and be sensitive to any variation of energy that you experience through holding the crystal.

CARING FOR SEED CRYSTALS

Under normal conditions, do not keep the seed

crystals near your other crystals. Maintain a separate place for storing them away from the vibrations of all others. Do not be concerned about others touching the seed crystal. They cannot alter or "invade" its frequencies. All that may occur is that they might be affected by the energies of the crystal.

Before we withdraw our vibrations, we give you a word of caution. There will be those who will attempt to profit unjustly from these written words. They will claim to have seed crystals for sale to you. Always be cautious and determine the validity with your own guidance. If there is any doubt in your mind, pass it by with love.

We are the Father, Mother, God. Blessings upon your souls.

The magnetic processes and knowledge of Atlantis are coming into your grasp in a rapid manner, and I wish to commend all of mankind for its continuing growth toward unity among all of My Children.

RELEASING ATLANTEAN KARMA

The Order of the evolution of the planet Earth is progressing according to the Divine Plan. The time has come for all those who have affected themselves with unresolved Atlantean karmic obligations to release them into My care. Only in this manner can you fulfill your current destinies upon Earth. I await your requests to fill this area of your needs.

The new Atlantis will not be as the old Atlantis. All precautions have been taken to insure that emotional expressions will never again destroy the spiritual Order of your planet Earth.

Those of you who have volunteered to serve again have endured, and will continue to endure conditioning of your reactive patterns a thousand times over to insure against their misuse. In the end, all you have endured will be returned to you tenfold in growth, peace, and happiness.

As time passes and it is seen that mankind is properly utilizing the knowledge that has been transcribed, more will be released into consciousness. Within thirty of your years, the lower karmic band of emotional expression will be released from involvement with the planet Earth. It will be replaced with growth and expansion frequencies of higher evolution.

This, in itself, will bring peace to mankind. No longer will people be involved in emotional patterns of destruction, abuse, and violation of others. Souls of those frequencies will no longer incarnate upon the planet Earth. They will re-enter elsewhere in continuing compatible vibrations.

The basic soul level on Earth will have changed and evolved to the new frequencies of your Age of Enlightenment. Be joyous and gratified, as the results of your efforts bear the fruit of the Garden of Eden, the planet Earth, the New Atlantis.

The Blessings of your Universe be with you.

6

This is Adamis, relating to you from the Creative quadrant of eternal existence of All.

It is time for Us to begin to relate to you a systematic program of devices to be utilized in the pursuit of your efforts for mankind. Some of these have been described to you before, in earlier writings. Now it is time for you to begin to use them in an active, prescribed manner.

HEALING GENERATOR

This device is an Atlantean healing generator. When assembled, the two healing leads will each be eight feet in length. Place the subject on a table in a prone position. Touch each lead in a position relating to an energy insertion point. This will establish the magnetic circuitry of polarity to correct the energy aberration.

The device may be used for healing of all conditions, with the exception of the physical heart and pure spiritual manifestations. It is constructed as follows:

Build a square box six inches in height and ten inches in length, using one-half-inch wood. Do not use synthetic materials.

Cut four one-half-inch copper tubes to this length, and secure as the diagram shows. Cut notches, one-half inch apart, in the exposed portion of each copper tube.

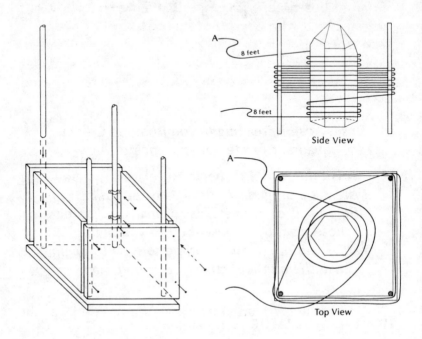

A ⌇ 8 feet

8 feet

Side View

A

Top View

Place three inches of natural grains, preferably rice, in the bottom of the box as aligning material to keep the crystal erect. Set a generator crystal of fourteen to eighteen inches in length in the grains in an erect position. Measure the length from the inside bottom of the box to the top of the exposed barrel of the crystal.

Leaving eight feet of twenty-guage copper wire, wind the wire around the base of the crystal, three times. Then proceed to wrap the wire around the copper tube in the notches until you reach the top of the barrel of the crystal. Wrap the wire around the crystal three more times and allow another eight feet of wire to remain free. The device is now ready for use.

The frequency of energy that is generated is quite intense. You are requested to use this device with caution, and to ascertain beforehand that the subject is not involved with any form of mechanical or electrical appliance on or in their bodies such as a pacemaker.

This application is extremely effective when dealing with a short-circuitry of energy flow that results in spasms or seizures.

METAFORMS™

The purpose of a Metaform™ is to help human beings grow through interaction with energy. Energy is catalytic in its nature, stirring up and stimulating growth, much as a seed is started in its process of becoming a plant by the warmth of the sun. Energy serves as a connector in communication with the higher self, as demonstrated by meditation, which allows information and understanding to flow through an individual. Thirdly, energy as the basis of all matter is capable of transforming the physical plane. This third point is one of the most powerful and difficult aspects of energy to explain, for we are saying here that an actual physical transformation can occur within a body by bathing it within a particular frequency of energy. Within a single Metaform™, such as the Aquarian Pyramid™, the choice of energies is widely varied.

The molecular and atomic matrix of matter reflects the unique geometric patterns of different energy frequencies/forms. A Metaform™, in mimicking this manifestation of energy on the macro level (our size), resonates with the particular energy. This is similar to a "C" tuning fork resonating with a "C" tone. Thus we are capable of experiencing a strong, pure concentration of energy in the Metaform.™*

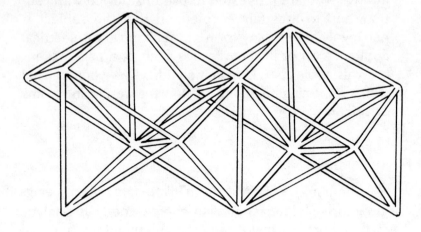

THE AQUARIAN PYRAMID

The device pictured on the following page is a three-dimensional copper Aquarian Pyramid™. It was used for many purposes during ancient Atlantean days. The base is in the form of the six-pointed star. The over structure converts it to a multidimensional energy corrective mechanism. Notice the six pyramids over the six points of the star.

*The Aquarian Pyramid and the three-dimensional Star of David have been constructed by Gregory Hoag. These have inspired him to create other copper devices that have been named "Metaforms.™" Both names, Aquarian Pyramid™ and Metaforms™, have been trademarked, and all devices are patent pending. If you desire any further information or a catalog of Metaforms™, contact Gregory Hoag, P.O. Box 2262, Boulder, Colorado 80306.

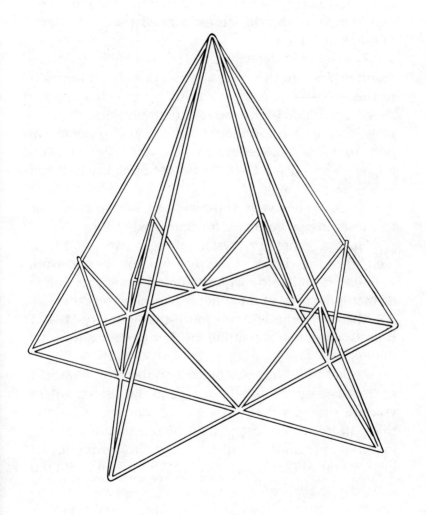

This device generates the same field of energy as the pattern of twelve crystals, the cause and effect energies assigned to the planet Earth.

Sit inside the device, either on the floor or on a low stool, and place yourself in a meditative position. You may remain in the device for a period of up to thirty minutes at a time.

The Aquarian Pyramid™ may be used in the following manner: You are the control energy. Assign a function to the energies of each of the six outer pyramids. We suggest these divisions—space communication, healing magnetics, ultra-color frequencies, spiritual communication, past life knowledge, and chakra alignment. You might wish to place a small card denoting the function inside each pyramid.

If your needs vary, you may assign other functions to these energy vortexes, for that is what they are.

Place a generator crystal (at least two pounds in weight) in the center of the pyramid you wish to work with. Lay it on its side with the point facing you. This is all that is necessary for the desired result to be achieved.

The only time you use more than one crystal at a time is when you are sitting inside the device for total energizing.

At that time, you may place a crystal or generator in each of the pyramids, all pointing to the center, where you are sitting. We strongly advise that you remain in this pattern for no longer than fifteen minutes. Sitting in this configuration will generate the frequency of energy that will also align your conscious mind with the energies of your soul.

THE ENERGY GRID

The copper energy grid has been described to you earlier in Our writings. On page 70 there is a diagram of its construction and the required materials.

We cannot over-stress the importance of this device during the adjustments you are making in this New Age. All karmic experiences are being speeded to completion. This must result in greater insecurities and unsettlement on your part. If you will construct this device, and use it for meditation by placing a pattern of twelve on its perimeter, it will serve to readjust your vibrations and keep them aligned with the rapidity of your growth.

The two leads of the generator device can be attached at the head and foot of the energy grid. This will create an all-over, even distribution of magnetics that is most effective in the treatment of arthritis, bursitis, nerve conditions, circulation problems, and skin conditions. It can also be used just to reenergize yourself from fatigue and stress of the physical body.

In all applications with devices, always remember that they are merely tools for your use. Do not allow yourself or anyone else to become overly dependent upon them. As your magnetic circuitry becomes completed, you may lay them aside. All you will need will be belief and mind control over your dissemination of energies.

It is strongly suggested that you do not expose children under the age of ten years to the grid system and the crystals in a pattern of twelve. A triangulation of three crystals will be compatible with the strength of their energy frequencies. Do not allow them to be exposed to the grid energies for longer than five of your minutes at a time.

COPPER ENERGY GRID

FOR MAXIMUM BENEFIT, LAY FLAT ON THIS GRID
WITHIN THE "PATTERN OF 12 CRYSTALS".
| CAUTION! | MAXIMUM TIME = 15 MINUTES.

LIST OF MATERIALS:
```
172 - 2" FINISHING NAILS (PLUS SOME FOR MISTAKES)
  8 - 3⅛" FLATHEAD NAILS
  2 - 3'-0" LONG  2×4 WOOD STUDS
  2 - 6'-2" LONG  2×4 WOOD STUDS
  2 SPOOLS (±25'-0" EA.)  20 GA. COPPER WIRE
```
LIST OF TOOLS:
```
    HAMMER
    PLIERS
    WIRE CUTTERS
```
DIRECTIONS:
1. ASSEMBLE WOOD FRAME AS SHOWN.   PLACE FINISHING
   NAILS 1¼" APART AND WEAVE COPPER WIRE AROUND
   NAILS AS SHOWN TO CREATE A GRID PATTERN. (SEE INSERT.)
2. CRIMP OR SOLDER INTERSECTION POINTS AS SHOWN.
3. REMOVE ENOUGH NAILS TO DETACH COPPER GRID FROM
   WOOD FRAME.
4. GRID MAY BE SEWN BETWEEN
   SHEETS FOR ADDED COMFORT

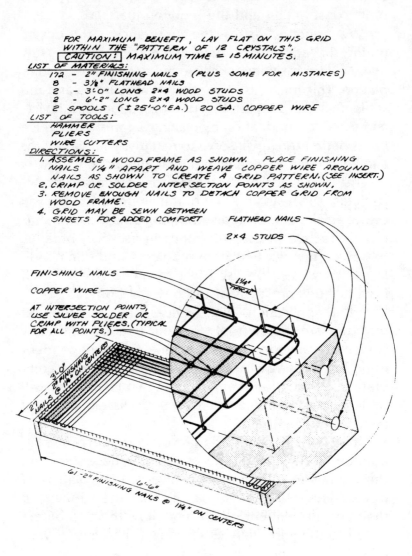

This is Pythagoras speaking.

OVERLAY PATTERNS

In the application of crystals for purposes of healing, there are many triangulation patterns that are applied directly on the physical body, with or without the placement of an outer pattern of crystals. These are referred to as "overlay patterns."

Chakras

The positioning of the crystals directly relates to the energy insertion and chakra positions in the physical body. To assist you in this, we will list these positions and their locations:

    1—Center of head at the hairline (Crown).
    2—Center of head, one inch above eyebrows
        (Third Eye).
    3—Center bottom of throat (Throat).
    4—Center of chest in line with physical body
        (Heart).
    5—Center, just below ribcage (Solar Plexus).

6—Center, four inches below navel (Spleen).

7—Base of spine (Base or Root).

8—Center, back top of head (Clairvoyance).

9—Center, base of skull where it rests on spine (Channeling).

11 & 12—Behind each ear in mastoid area.

13 & 14—Top of each shoulder directly over armpit.

15 & 16—Inside bend of each elbow.

17 & 18—Center of the palm of each hand.

19 & 20—Top center of each hip.

21 & 22—Top of the thigh of each leg where it joins the trunk of the body.

23 & 24—Inside the bend of each knee.

25 & 26—Center of the ball of each foot.

27 & 28—Back center of each thigh where it meets the buttocks.

29—Spine, in the small of the back.

30—Spine, in line with the navel.

31 & 32—Center of each shoulder-blade on the back.

Energy Insertion Points

The energy insertion points are as follows:

1 & 2—In the center of each ear opening.

3 & 4—One inch directly behind the corner of each eye.

5 & 6—One inch above the top of the earlobe on each side of the head.

7 & 8—Balancing points inside collarbone on each side of neck.

9—The tips of all fingers and toes.

10—On both sides of each elbow.

11—On both sides of each knee.

12—On both sides of each ankle.

13 & 14—On the inside of each arm at the wrist.

15—The navel.

Treatments Utilizing Overlay Patterns

These chakra and energy insertion points are the anchors for all overlay patterns applied to the surface of the physical body. Examples of treatments utilizing the chakra and energy insertion points are as follows:

A. For treatment of upper respiratory conditions or any problems in the upper torso, place a crystal on each shoulder and one on the navel. All points are facing the center of the triangle.

B. For treatment of any condition in the lower portion of the torso, place a crystal on the top center of each thigh, and one on the solar plexus chakra; all points face inward.

C. For arthritis in the elbow, place one crystal on the shoulder, one on the inside of the elbow, and one in the center of the palm.

This process can be utilized in conjunction with the pattern of six or the pattern of twelve crystals. The ultimate overlay pattern is described as follows:

Have the person lie down, face up. Place the crystals in the following positions on the body all points upward.

- In the palm of each hand.
- On top of each thigh chakra.
- Over the root chakra.
- On the navel.
- Over the heart chakra.
- On the throat chakra.
- On each shoulder chakra.
- On the crown chakra.

You have set in place a total of eleven crystals. The subject is the twelfth, the completion. This application will correct and balance any energy disturbances in the body and relieve all blockages. It will also bring into conscious sensation all causes of emotional distress and self-judgment. Do not leave anyone alone while this process is taking place. Under normal conditions, there will be some emotional reactions requiring support and reassurance.

As always, what we have described to you is not the only method of these applications. Use your own minds. Tune into your own guidance, and you will be directed to additional methods of applying overlay patterns for healing in all areas of expression.

ENERGY IMPLANTS AND ADJUSTMENTS

Before Atlantis was destroyed, those Elders who had elected to serve as the core beings on the surface of Earth were transported aboard ship for specific energy implants and adjustments. These processes were necessary in order to enable the physical beings to retain spacial communication with the assigned ships that were to be their guidance control.

History will repeat itself. It is not too many years away when those same souls will be taken aboard ship once again for this same conscious process. This time, the control and dissemination of energies will be under the frequencies of the Golden Triad Rays of Creative Light. We will now share with you from the source of these energies.

Welcome to the Creative Mass, for this is the source of the energies that share with you at

this time. Through the stream of these energies, universes are created and voids in the Mass of Creation are filled with Light. Through these prismatic patterns of Light, frequencies are transmitted to souls throughout Creation, in all universes, for their growth and evolution as souls and parts of the Whole.

THE ATLANTEAN TABLETS

It has been deemed time to begin to relate to mankind some of the information contained on the ancient Atlantean Tablets. It is to that purpose that these energies are with you now.

Ramtos

A void in the Mass was assigned for the Creation of a new Universe. Energies from the Mass were directed through the frequencies of the Golden Triad to be properly magnetized and projected into place. A new Universe had been conceived. A new source for adding dimensions and growth to All had been created.

The expressive resonance for this Universe was, and is, "RAMTOS" in your language and vibrationary correlation.

This selection of frequencies resulted in the following patterns of expression for all souls to be incarnated within that Universe. These frequencies encourage all souls to seek the eternal Oneness in Love with the God, Creator, assigned to this monumental task. They set a pattern of expression in growth of strength, softness, expansion, and fulfillment, so the creation of perpetual evolution was set into motion once again.

The Four Quadrants

The four directive quadrants were set into place, and the creation of souls commenced. The evolutionary process, until the formation of the planet you know as Earth, took untold eons of your time. Within your Universe of Ramtos, there are millions of galaxies, and tens of quadrillions of planets. All are in varying stages of evolution and settlement.

The planet Earth was designated to be vibrationally attuned to the resonance of "ALTA," to have the power, the expansion, and the resilience of the highest Order. It was to this end that the Atlanteans settled on Earth when their planet became uninhabitable. Many cycles of expression have risen and been completed. Now, at this time, the destiny of the planet Earth can be fulfilled at last.

Projections in the form of World Teachers are incarnated on Earth from the four quadrants of Creative existence. They are among you now, and will remain in physical expression until World Unity has become a reality.

Seeds of Achievement

The "seeds" of achievement planted upon the planet Earth were those who volunteered from many quadrants to be part of the Atlantean reconstruction. You who walk with open minds and hearts are those "seeds." Your God calls you "shepherds." It does not matter, for from you will blossom the fruit of fulfillment for the "All" of Creation.

Energy Structures on Earth

Before Atlantis was destroyed, there were four World sites selected to house World energies and information relating to the future of Earth. One of these is located in the Himalaya Mountains. One is the Great Pyramid in Egypt. One is a mountain of magnetics in the State of Arizona, and the last is located in New Zealand. Structures of pure energy were set into place over these designated areas. Through the vibrations of the Golden Triad Light, rigid patterns of geometric frequencies were implanted into the energy structures. This information contains the tools for the total enlightenment of mankind.

Bear in mind that the four structures exist today as they have always existed—as pure energy. They will never be destroyed for as long as this planet exists. Through quite intricate mathematical formulae, information is gradually released into the surrounding strata of energy relating to the planet Earth. From this point, whenever mankind reaches another level of growth and evolution, it triggers a release of frequencies of higher evolution to be attained.

Creative Relativity

The formula for this process of Creative Relativity is $C = 4Q + U^7$. A simple explanation would be: Assimilation into Creation equals the four quadrants of energy mass added to the seventh power of the Universe.

The Atlanteans used the information dispensed through the Golden Triad to advance their civilizations and then to destroy them. Do not allow this to occur again. They became aware of Universal keys to genetic construction and, through their experiments, brought forth beings of greatly distorted energy frequencies. The minds of these beings emitted such a great field of negative frequencies that the balance of energies became badly distorted. This, of course, contributed to the downfall of Atlantis.

Maintaining the Order

Your God has created everything in Divine Order, in compatibility with Universal consciousness. It is not in order for mankind to interrupt a flow that could have effects in other worlds and civilizations. Try to allow incarnated beings the full expression of their souls. It is not in order to interfere with the plan of karmic incarnation as determined by your God.

When it is in order, the knowledge and availability of the Light of the Golden Triad will be with you.

The ultimate functions and purposes for healing with magnetics through the application of crystals has begun to change. This change in purpose will become increasingly important as the masses of mankind begin to come into their awareness.

USE OF CRYSTALS FOR EVOLUTION

To this point, we have concentrated on crystal applications relating to physical maintenance, not evolution. All of this will change as awareness and recognition of the value of the physical structure come to mankind. The body should retain health and life for hundreds of your years. As you become aware of this, physical healing will become unnecessary and outdated.

Healing, by universal definition, means: "The perpetuation of eternal forces of existence relating to energy." Once again, we bring you a new definition on the spirals of evolution of understanding and acceptance.

The use for your crystals will drastically change—not now, but in several decades. The physical body is, in essence, a tool for the spiritual energies to express. Therefore, once acknowledged, God can heal all physical disorders—all of them. This means that you can heal all physical disorders once you acknowledge that you are as God. A thought heals. A word heals. Acceptance heals. Too much emphasis is placed on the healing processes of the physical body. The more ritual and exercises you are involved in, the less faith and belief you are demonstrating.

Once again, crystals are the magnetic vehicles of the Universe. They are the working, conductive energies of containment and evolution. Through their applications, they are a tool for conscious development, by affording the mind the opportunities to explore other areas of existence and amplification of frequencies.

USING YOUR CRYSTALS FOR ADJUSTMENT OF ENERGIES

We have stated to you that the karmic bands of expression currently assigned to Earth are going to be changed. The lower band of heavy emotional experience will be removed. It is for this purpose that you will mainly be using your crystals to help the adjustment in the energy meridians of the physical structure, and re-adapt them for continuing compatibility with the Earth planet.

The following is an example of the process that you will be involved in: Someone comes to you in a very distraught condition. He is having problems just living. He is feeling that there is no peace or place for him. He is nervous and uncomfortable most of the time. He does not seem to be able to concentrate and achieve anything worthwhile. (These will become commonplace statements to you in a few of your years.)

The causes for this condition must be understood. The planet Earth has evolved into new frequencies as part of its evolution. Those who are still "spiritually asleep" will not be compatible with the new energies, and the forementioned conditions will arise for them. If something is not done for them, their world will become a shambles, for they will find no peace. This is one of the prime functions for your applications with crystals.

It has been deemed in Order for you to move these individuals through levels of karmic expression in shorter periods of time. (They called this pre-programming in Atlantis.) You commence by explaining the causes for these conditions to the individual. You must then explain your purpose and intent. If they are not in accord with your intent, pass them by, and allow them to be as they have chosen. Do not ever impose this program on anyone. If all is in order, proceed in the following manner:

Have the person lie down on his back, and begin to move your hands over his body in circular fashion. (Direction is unimportant.) Do this for at least five minutes. This action stimulates the magnetic flow of energies in the body and prepares him for added stimulation and insertion.

Place a crystal over each of the seven basic chakras, with the points all facing toward the head. Connect the energy flow seven times, and allow the individual to lie there and experience this for ten minutes. Remove the crystals and talk to him. He will have experienced some degree of insecurity. Urge him to share it with you, and counsel him accordingly. When peace has been established, continue in the following manner:

Tape a crystal to the chakra on the center of the ball of each foot. Place a crystal in the palm of each hand, point upward. Place a crystal on the chakra on each shoulder, point downward. Place a crystal over the heart chakra, point upward. Now, take a crystal in your hand (larger than the ones you placed on the body), and slowly moe it over the body until you have connected the circuitry. When you feel the circuitry has become completed, allow the person to remain in this pattern for ten minutes. When the treatment is completed, remove the crystals and allow him to rest quietly for awhile. Sit him up and have him relate to you once again.

This concludes the first stage of treatment. Tell him that, if he feels anything uncomfortable, to call you and speak to you. This is most important, for he will experience uneasiness and additional insecurities.

Remember, you are beginning the causing of change. As the person becomes aware of the energy, he will experience a change, and it may make him feel insecure.

The second treatment may take place a week later. Place the subject lying down once again. Set up a pattern of twelve crystals around him, and leave him in the pattern for ten minutes. When this time has elapsed, activate the green crystal implants in the palms of your hands. Place them on the shoulders of the person, and move them down the entire length of the body. Do this three times. The person will still be in the pattern of twelve when you are doing this.

You may repeat this treatment every other day, for a series of seven treatments. After the completion of each treatment, allow the person to rest for awhile. This permits the energies to become distributed, and will not cause disorientation.

Now your work has truly begun. The individual will slowly begin to change, and experience early forms of awareness. It is most important that he has someone to talk to.

Otherwise, he will close the doors in fear and lack of understanding. Keep in close contact, and answer his questions, and he will begin to grow.

This process of frequency alteration will open the minds of mankind. The need for this treatment will increase daily, as more and more people become aware of energy changes around them. Your existence is mind. If you place the mind in order, the body will place itself in order.

You will use the crystals to open the chakras of clairvoyance and of channeling. These centers are naturally associated with magnetic frequencies. By placing two crystals near the chakras, they will amplify the frequency receptivity of these centers. Treatment may be given as often as desired, but never for longer than several minutes at a time.

Blessings.

8

*These are the energies of Pythagoras
sharing with you.*

THE TREE OF LIFE

The formula $C = 4Q + U^7$ pertains to the ultimate evolution of the energy force created in eternal frequency as a soul. The Kabalistic Tree of Life representation is the result of strong Atlantean influences and souls. What of the "Tree of Life" of the Hindus, the Moslems, the Buddhists? Is there only one Kabala, or is there more than one?

The Atlanteans did not speak of God. They spoke only of the magnetic order of the Universe. These same souls, when incarnated as Hebrews, spoke only of God. What transpired to cause this change in consciousness?

In Atlantis, the Book of Law was called the "JOBAL," the Magnetic Order of the Universe. This brought Atlanteans into acceptance of creative eternity of energy, the soul. It gave them the mathematical understanding of the multiplication of energy as an additive process resulting from evolution and growth. The more energy one absorbs, the greater power one possesses.

As a result of this, much time was devoted to experiments involving methods of energy amplification and absorption. This resulted in the invention of many devices and uses for energy that you have available to you today. However, in the application of science, one must always leave room for the catalyst, spiritual intangibles, or God.

The Atlanteans did not do this, and it, above all else, led to the destruction of their civilization. Within all action and reaction, all expressions of balance and counterbalance, all exercises of cause and effect, there is a catalyst. The catalyst is always God. Anything else is karmic, for it is a variable. God is the only constant, the only reality to relate to.

The "4Q" in the formula pertains to the four Creative quadrants of energy that compose this Universe, Ramtos. From these quadrants are derived the stimulating karmic frequencies of experience pertaining to planetary incarnated life. All souls created within a Universe are derived from the energies of one of these quadrants, even though they are created by God. All must experience God. All must experience magnetics. All must experience Universal Love. All must experience total Brotherhood.

These are the core energies of the "Quadrantial Trees of Life"—not one, but four, leading into *Oneness* with the Creative Mass. Every soul, in the course of its existence, is exposed to the energies and experiences of all four quadrants. However, each is only a derivative of one. This is what maintains the balance of cause-and-effect energies within a given Universe.

THE "ORDER"

The creation of soul is always in total order. Expressions are created to achieve balance, not numerical superiority. There is not a soul created for power and control, only for balance.

The Atlantean Elders were all part of the same quadrant, that of magnetics. On their own planet, they survived and evolved in total harmony and peace. However, when they came to the planet Earth, it was a different matter. This planet contained the vibrations of God Acceptance, of Love, of Brotherhood, and what you call emotional response and reactions.

The souls began to experience the emotional, karmic frequencies of self-adulation and adornment. Gone were the attempts to reach beyond the simple reactive capacities. They were satisfied to relate their total existence within their physical lives. As time elapsed, their minds closed to the universal frequencies. It was as if they placed a closed door into the flow of eternal knowledge and existence. Here and there, an isolated few maintained their oneness with the energies of their Creation. They were called Seers and Prophets.

The "Order" must be explained. When the souls of the Elders of Atlantis incarnated on the surface of Earth, their mission was to form twelve divisions of expressions. Your Bibles call them the "Twelve Tribes of Israel." They were physically dispersed throughout the corners of your World to establish a variety of cultures, paths to God, etc.—to create a balance of expression.

The planet Earth had been cleansed. New karmic bands of experience had been set into place to assure the conscious evolution of mankind. It was not intended for man to ignore the energies beyond Earth, but that is what occurred.

The energies of emotions, greed, power, fear, doubt, and carnal expression became the overlay of oppression for the soul.

Look at your own lives. When you allow yourselves emotional distress, does it not cloud your ability to relate to your higher attitudes of expression? That is what took place on a much larger scale and to an intense degree.

Most of the karmic responsibility that you have begun to recall relates to this period, not to Atlantis, for it was here that the "doors" closed and service came to a halt.

From the moment the resettlement began on Earth, the ships were in attendance to assist in the reconstruction. It was not the purpose to begin at the beginning, but to continue forward from the last level of expression. This never came to pass. The ships withdrew, for they could not interfere with the free-will vibrations assigned to the planet Earth, and the "doors" to the souls continued to close consciously.

In the final course of Divine Order, all must come to pass. As the vibrations of the Piscean Era began to wane and the first senses of the Aquarian Age began to be expressed, things began to change. The societies of Earth began to experience revolutions and rebellions relating to personal freedom and expression. The "Beatniks," the "Hippies," and the "Flower Children" appeared all over your World. These expressions were totally in order, for they were the seeds of awakening the soul in relation to the conscious mind.

The Age of Enlightenment is with you. It has appeared a full cycle later in expression than intended, almost 9,000 years, but it is here at last. Now, mankind has created other problems. You have wars, but are they wars for greed, power, and control? Are they not expressions to obtain freedom from greed, power, and control? Perhaps they are another form of cleansing and the last vestiges of the Piscean Age, of the "sword of power," as the energies of universal magnetics begin to burst forth into the consciousness of mankind.

THE SEVEN DIVISIONS OF ENERGY FREQUENCIES

Part of the formula is written "U^7." This refers to the seven main divisions of the spiraling frequencies of energy that comprise this Universe, Ramtos. We will now discuss these levels in relation to Atlantean times, as well as to your Aquarian Age.

We begin this discussion with the seven frequency levels of a vibration called "LOVE."

1. Soul Acknowledgement of Self-Existence

The creation of a soul involves the geometric assimilation of three vibrations of energy into a unit called a soul. The total existence of the soul involves the multiplication of these vibrations into one unitized mass of Light. These vibrations are masculine, feminine, and love.

When the soul is created, it must learn to assimilate these vibrations into oneness and acknowledge its existence as a viable part of that Universe. It cannot love one part of itself more than the others. This process is the first spiritual karmic expression pattern of the soul.

2. Soul Acknowledgement of God as Its Creator

Universal Law states, "Once a soul acknowledges the existence of God, it cannot ever deny this reality." This is the first external expression of the frequencies of Love.

It allows the soul to experience the vibrations of an eternal force other than itself.

Perhaps this experience is the most vital to the soul,

for it sets the patterns for later acceptance of other souls in their own frequencies and identities. The soul learns that it is part of the God force of Light, and yet it is unique unto itself and is self-contained.

3. Emotional Expression of: Ownership, Attachment, Commitment, Sacrifice, Guilt, Punishment, and Lack of Individuality

This is the first frequency level that involves a physical expression, and a conscious mind and personality. It is here that the soul is often the "victim" of the conscious mind, and karmic conditions are created that affect the soul. The dealing with these frequencies was established as part of the karmic pattern for the planet Earth, for this area is the foundation for the next four levels of expression.

The Atlantean civilization was a caste system of expressions. The lower castes were evolving through these vibrations, but the Elders had achieved consciousness and understanding. Their previously described methods of union were proof of this achievement.

When settlement occurred on the surface of Earth, exposure to the lower karmic frequencies clouded this spiral of expression. The struggle of mankind to rid itself of all superlatives relating to Love is the most complex of all Earthly experiences. Mankind has been conditioned into sacrifice, etc. Now you are being impressed with universal magnetic vibrations, and a measure of uncertainty and confusion has entered your reactive systems.

This also occurred in Atlantis. The genetic experiments "opened the carnal doors" in the expressions of many of the Elders. One could say that a form of regression took place, and a continuing pattern had been triggered.

Many Atlantean souls have allowed themselves to fall into this pattern of discord during their current lifetimes. Think about this, and see if you have followed this pattern in the past. This attitude must be relieved, and it is coming to pass. Your methods of union are being challenged. Your form of relationships is being pressured into expressions of change and reformation.

The pure definition of "Love" at this level is the "acceptance of all conditions that seem to be reality for this moment." It has nothing to do with emotions at all. In order to complete the third frequency level, it is necessary to accept your existence totally as an expression of an eternal soul, nothing more. If you can achieve this, all will fall into place for you.

Your current attitude toward your physical body, and its expression and appearance is quite archaic. Please try to remember that the physical body and all of its expressions represent a vehicle through which your soul evolves. Begin to release the purely emotional and sexual attitudes, and use your body as a completion factor of love expressed by your soul.

4. Conscious Worthiness of Self and Soul

Until the release of pure emotional love expression has been accomplished, the worthiness of soul and self cannot be achieved. In effect, what we are saying is that all—and we mean all—judgments of yourself must end in every expression. The heart must open to self in total acknowledgment and acceptance. You must rise above the generations of conditioning in growth and peace. You are expression of soul, and cannot be unworthy in any aspect of universal existence.

True love is acceptance of self and soul; then you can allow others to experience who you are. The important fact is that you only allow them to experience you by sharing of yourself, not by giving in sacrifice. If mankind will begin to practice this process, the destruction of Atlantis will never again be repeated. Everyone will acknowledge the total worthiness of their sisters and brothers, and will accept them or not accept them into their lives, accordingly.

5. Universal Love of All

Reach out into the Universe with your mind, experience the energies of total sameness, and all has come to pass. Yet, in physical form, your ego judges. Your former unworthiness creates blocks in your development. If you have reached this fifth step, then you know that all are the same, created from the same geometric formula of energy.

This perception of Love totally relates to the unqualified acceptance of everyone's right to be as they wish to be. It also means that your spiritual Masters are as you, that the Ascended Masters are as you, that the Hierachy is as you. All are part of the Creative expression and are the same.

This is Universal Love, not an emotional experience that qualifies your every move, thought, and expression. Love all souls as yourself. Allow them to be who they desire to be.

6. Symbolic Release of the Soul, God

Mankind on Earth today is involved in a magnetic awakening that is causing people to open the doors of their minds. They are climbing aboard the spiral of Light that will lead them into the destiny of their souls.

Part of this process is the symbolic release of the soul serving as God, Creator of this Universe. This release involves nothing more than the acknowledgment that something exists beyond this Universe. I am talking about letting go of God as the limit of your evolution and total existence.

The source of the energy that God used to create your soul comes from the quadrants of energy that are part of the Mass of the Creative Force of All. Reach for this. Allow yourself your worthiness to go beyond. In doing so, you are ready for completion of the vibrations of Love, the Creative acceptance.

7. Creative Acceptance

Here you are, walking on Earth, and your mind is absorbing twenty thoughts and conversations at the same time. What has happened? You seem to be here, and yet not here. People tell you that "you" have visited them during the night to speak, and you are unaware of the visit.

All of the above is truth and Creative acceptance of Love. All of the above will come to pass for you. All of the above are aspects of your Creative Tree of Life under the frequencies of *Love*.

ROJANI

I, Pythagoras, walked in Atlantis under the name of "Rojani." I created many of the highly sophisticated computers to a degree beyond your present conceptions. I saw and participated in the expressions of lack of universal love and acceptance. I tried to create programs to counter these expressions, with no success. I saw the end coming, and was unable to stop it from taking place. Perhaps I too could not see beyond my eyes.

If only the Atlanteans, myself included, had not allowed their souls to be clouded by their conceptions of love, what a world you would have at this time. It is not too late, for there is no time, only existence. Learn, sisters and brothers, learn, and bring your Age of Enlightenment into reality for all mankind, and for God.

During my early Atlantean days, I was involved in many unions of vibrations, what you call marriages. There were times when the compatible energies dissipated, leaving us no choice but to dissolve the unions.

What would have occurred if we had assumed your attitudes and suffered, stifling our individual selves by allowing emotional fears to force us to remain together? Nothing, only sacrifice on both our parts.

For the most part, Atlantean relationships did not involve the interchange of emotions. They did involve the exchange of mind frequencies and compatible vibrational areas of expression. In this manner, all relationships were most productive and stimulating. We never tired, for the constant mental interchange always renewed the energy union, and growth resulted for all.

The highest frequency definition for the word "relationship" is "the constant growth resulting from compatible interchange of energy." This is the eternal key, and the universal vibration of evolution in this expression.

EMOTIONS AS CAUSES OF CONFLICTS

Two civilizations, Atlantis and Lemuria, both existed during the same period of time. These civilizations were quite similar in nature and purpose. They were to be the balancing expressions of all interactions, one east and one west. Souls interchanged incarnations in both civilizations to experience both cultures and their methods of expression. But, if this was the case, why did they periodically fight with each other?

There is no pure universal answer, only an emotional one, for emotions were the sole cause for the conflicts.

As long as souls have—and will physically incarnate with—emotional capabilities, they will always have choice. Another way to phrase this would be with your words, "temptation, or negative selection of action." Without this, emotional karmic experiences could not exist, for there would be no decisions to make or to be responsible for.

Each time the Lemurians or Atlanteans developed a new concept or application, their relationships suffered as thoughts of control affected their thought patterns. Each time one felt inferior to the other, uprisings, in the guise of battles, took place. In the end, their relationship was dissolved, and destruction was the victor.

The soul who walked on Earth as Adolph Hitler served as an Elder of Lemuria. During that time, the personality succumbed to the temptations of power and control. History repeats itself until all experiences are learned. Most of those on your planet who express the negatives of power and greed have expressed them in the past, and have not rectified the vibrational frequency.

Are you to blame them and judge them, or is it in order to blame those who allowed these relationships to take place? Why do you not blame the followers, the ones who carried out the destruction and search for power and control? You must consider these words. Then you must examine all of your relationships in truth.

Ask yourself some questions:

- Are both being served in this relationship?
- Am I involved in sacrifice in order to be served?
- Is this relationship one of choice, or the result of pressure from others?
- What is the foundation for this relationship?

- Is this relationship still viable, or has it become only a comfortable habit?

If you are an Atlantean, know that you have the strength in your soul to rectify your life in this area. If you wish to maintain a relationship that is not in total order, admit it to yourself, and you will not suffer from it. Truth is the answer, truth to yourself.

Blessings.

9

This is Adamis. Blessings to you.

FREQUENCIES OF CRYSTALS

Each crystal carries its own frequency of energies. This is geometrically determined by size, length, angles of facets, and the width of the sides. The Atlanteans had the ability to create, in perfection, the sizes needed for their functions. This also determined the exact frequencies of energy. At this time, mankind is not capable of this.

When acquiring a crystal, always compare the frequencies with your own energies. If a disparity is present, seek out another. (You could invest the time required to alter the vibrations, but it could be very time-consuming for you.) Bless the crystal, and determine the function for which it will serve—healing, communication, or education.

CRYSTALS FOR EDUCATION

We will now discuss the utilization of crystals for education.

In an earlier volume, we described the process by which children in Atlantis were taught—the placing of leads on the head from previously programmed crystals that implanted energy vibrations in the brain. At this time, you are not ready to accept this process, nor do you have the proper technology available to you. However, there are other methods that you can utilize productively.

At this time, and for the next decade, Atlantean souls and other highly evolved souls will be incarnating on the planet Earth in increasing numbers. These children are the future of the Age of Enlightenment, and there will be vast numbers of them coming into physical incarnations.

When a woman becomes aware that she is with child, it is in order for her to begin a search for a communication crystal for the child. It must be totally compatible with her vibrations. She is to touch her body with the crystal, and receive input from the soul of the unborn child relating to choice. Once selected, this crystal is not to be used for anything else, nor is it to be touched by outside vibrations. It is to be kept apart from all other crystals and conductors of energy. In this manner, the frequency of receptivity will be maintained.

The crystal should be at least seven inches in length. This will be a strong enough amplifier to achieve the desired results. The purpose is to bring the crystal into harmony with the vibrations of the child's soul. Use the crystal in this manner several times weekly in the following manner: When the child has been born, sew the crystal into a soft covering, and leave it in the place where the child stays. The purpose for the covering is solely to protect the child from the edges of the crystal. It will not hamper the energy transfer.

As soon as the child is responsive, begin to show it the crystal and allow it to touch and become familiar with it. This will initiate the conscious flow of magnetics through the child's energy meridians. As time passes, acquaint the child with other crystals, and use them together. Set the conditions that the crystals are a normal part of daily use and expression. In this manner, acceptance of magnetics as a part of life's expression will become set in the child's mind at an early age.

Acquire another generator of approximately ten pounds. This will be the education amplifier for the child, as a crystal of that size has the capacity to store a high level of knowledge frequencies.

Sit at a table and place both hands on the crystal. Set the conditions that your energy thoughts are to be implanted in the crystal through your hands, and commence the dispensing of knowledge. Begin to "tell yourself a story." Relate the creation of the soul and all of the knowledge and philosophy in your mind. It will be as if you are teaching a class and the generator is your student. Implant all of your knowledge into the generator.

"Teach" the generator the English alphabet, and your child will begin to read at an early age. Picture the letters and associated objects in your mind; i.e., "A" and "Apple," and so on. Whatever you wish the child to be made aware of can be accomplished. You may begin this process of "teaching" the generator at any time. The energies will remain inside until they are consciously removed.

When the child has control over its movements and can be ambulatory, acquaint it with the generator. Train the child to hold onto the generator with its hands. The child may be watching television, or otherwise visually occupied, at the same time. The energies will begin to be transferred to the child's brain, and its education will commence.

It is of great importance to fully understand the purpose for this program of education. In the evolving of Earth's energies, it is no longer necessary for the closing of the "veil of knowledge" in newborn children. The aim is to keep the connection of soul to conscious mind open from birth. If this can be accomplished, much time will be saved, and mankind will move closer to fulfillment at a much more rapid pace.

Expose your child to information about Atlantis. Hang pictures near its crib. Purchase children's books and tapes, and whatever else is available to you. Insure that the spiritual development of your child is accomplished in a normal manner. Do not allow the child to feel that it is something "special," but make all aspects of growth appear to be the normal process of maturing. This will create security in the mind of the child and solidify its acceptance of this aspect of its expression.

What we have stated to you may seem revolutionary, but always remember that nothing is new. All we are concerned with is the awareness of energy that has always existed.

The implantation of energy in crystals and the resulting transferral of this energy to another is, of course, telepathic communication. The mind will become conditioned, and control will be established to enhance all forms of energy reception. It will open your mind and channels to spirit, to magnetics, and to the energies of God.

Begin to involve yourself in this process. Establish an energy center in your home, and place a generator there. Work in conjunction with one or several people, and commence the learning process of implanting and removing the vibrations of communication.

Always remember that dedication and devotion to purpose establishes the spiritual validity of a need. Only then can it become fulfilled. There is no easy path to enlightenment.

OTHER USES FOR THE GENERATOR DEVICE

The generator healing device can also be utilized for communication and energy thought transferral. When using it for communication, place one of the leads on your chakra for channeling, located at the base of your skull, and the other lead on your throat chakra. This will create a circuitry of reception and expression.

When using it to remove information, place the leads on the energy insertion points located one inch above the ears. You may not become consciously aware of the knowledge immediately. However, rest assured that the energies have been received by your brain and will come into consciousness slowly. They may come as casual thoughts, ideas, etc., but they will come to you and your awareness.

This form of learning and expression is an inherent part of the future of mankind. We ask you not to treat it lightly, but with sincerity and dedication.

The children of Atlantean Elders did not face the obstacles you faced, or that your children will face. They grew up in an aura of acceptance and development as eternal beings and aspects of universal existence.

PROGRAMS FOR CHILD DEVELOPMENT

Remember what you endured as a child. Remember all of the feelings of being alone, of being different, and being forced to keep the truth of your mind to yourself.

This cannot occur for your children. If it does, progress will be delayed. To help prevent this, consider the following programs that we suggest to you for now and for the future.

1. The establishment of a network of the parents of spiritual children. This is to be for the parents, not the children. It is for you to establish and exchange communication of ideas, problems, methods of teaching the children, obstacles that arise, and so on. This will create a support system that will serve as a constant stimulus for the parents to be committed to the growth of their children.

2. Establish growth classes for the children in your area. They are ready for this exposure when they reach five years of age, sometimes earlier, depending on the individual child. Alternate locations, class leaders, etc., among the parents to create an atmosphere of commitment, unity, and—most of all—responsibility.

Teach them in their own terminology. Seek out printed matter in your bookstores that will assist them and retain their interest and attention. Meditate with them, and—most important—share with them and encourage them to share with you.

3. The most important action to be taken is the establishment of childrens' spiritual ranches or camps during the summer months. They can be for a duration of several weeks, or longer if desired. This will bring the children together under conditions that are optimum for growth.

Look at yourselves. Do you not grow the most and feel more fulfilled when you are together with your sisters and brothers? Allow this feeling of security to develop in your children.

Establishment of these camps is strongly desired by the year of 1986. Put efforts into contacting teachers and others of like minds, and begin the process of fulfilling this method of child development.

It has been said that, if Order prevails, within three decades, the public school system will be teaching areas of spiritual development. The spiritual ranches are one of the keys to the fulfillment of these words.*

We are Pythagoras.

LOVE STARS

When Atlantis was destroyed, the resulting explosions and Earth changes cast many objects upon the surface of the planet. Among these objects were crystals known as "Love Stars" by the Atlanteans.

---

*If you are interested in participating in any of these programs, contact the Arizona Metaphysical Society, 3639 E. Clarendon, Phoenix, AZ 85018, or telephone (602) 956-1676, and they will supply you with further information concerning the forthcoming network.

These crystals grew in Atlantis as you grow flowers. Their unusual shape made them objects of beauty and love. They were given as bouquets of flowers, and exchanged as expressions of love when unions took place. They were also used for healing of conditions related to all aspects of emotional distress and unworthiness.

The crystals were clear and without color, but often seemed to reflect the softest pale blue light.

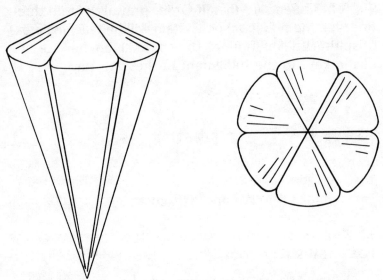

Today, the crystals are in a total state of shock. They are fully clouded with tears of sadness and grief. When one holds a "Love Star" to the breast, tears come into the eyes, as one becomes aware of the energies of sadness therein.

The crystals are found in clusters, many of them broken and shattered. They are located several feet below the surface of the Earth in the southeast portion of this country. If you are fortunate enough to have one of these "Love Stars" in your possession, you will treasure it always.

These crystals are never to be sold, only shared in love. An exchange can be tendered, if desired, but if one offers to sell you a Love Star, walk away, for it is not—and will not—be In Order.

Before Love Stars can be of service to you, you must be of service to them. The pain and energies of anguish must be transmuted and removed. Surround them in rose petals of soft pink vibrations, and heal them with energy on a daily basis. In time, the clarity will begin to return. When the clarity can be noticed, you may use them once again for service.

FUNCTIONS OF LOVE STARS

Their prime function for mankind is to reawaken the "sleeping" Atlantean minds. This means the negative aspects, as well as the positive aspects. The process is to place the Love Star over the spiritual third eye for two minutes. Have the subject relate consistently their feelings and experiences as they occur.

The second step is to place the crystal over the heart chakra. This allows the release to God of all negative energies that have been buried in the recesses of reactive patterns. In other words, the Love Star is to be used as a transformation crystal for all Atlantean expressions.

Universal Law tells you that action in a positive direction negates the vibrations in the opposite expression. By using the Love Star to heal others, you remove the energies of suffering from the crystal as well.

Once the Love Star has been cleared, it can be used as a source of information. They contain much knowledge energy from the Atlantean Era that can be released to you under the proper conditions.

The Love Stars will only come into the possession of Atlantean souls. All others will turn from their energies, and find them undesirable. In this manner, they will never be in the possession of the wrong people. What is meant by this statement is that, at any given moment, all energies are not developed to the same frequency of expression. Energies must be compatible before they can be equated with service.

Within the vibrations of existence and evolution is a geometric causation of energy reactions. These are noted as solar, galactic, and universal karmic experiences of evolution. In the existence of the soul during its universal confinement, all experiences in these pattern fields must be endured. Without this completion, the soul will not have the vibrational frequencies to transcend "universal confinement."

SOUL MASTERY

Each aspect involves a progressive system of experiences leading to understanding and assimilation of Universal Law. The initial aspect of expression involves what you call physical expression and the assimilation of planetary and natural vibrations, emotions, and spiritual essence into harmonic frequencies.

This process involves the duration of life and experiences from the creation of a soul until it achieves what you call physical expression and the assimilation of planetary and natural vibrations, emotions, and spiritual essence into harmonic frequencies.

This process involves the duration of life and experiences from the creation of a soul until it achieves what you call "soul mastery." This achievement brings the soul into frequencies that have the power to integrate into galactic expressions and service.

For the most part, the souls of the Atlantean Elders had achieved completion of the first aspect of evolution. This is important for you to understand, for only in this manner can you begin to accept fully the evolution and abilities of your souls.

We have related to you that the Elders were expressions in magnetic frequencies. Those in this expression had completed the energies of the "Order of Relationship to God." Another way to state this would be to say that the soul has established a working relationship with God. The soul understands the lack of need for adoration in servitude, unworthiness, and so on. It knows that all are parts of all, and that all work in unison and harmony.

The emotional cloak creates insecurities in this aspect of truth. It causes doubts relating to the validity of God, and even to God's existence. Your Earthly religions have served to further create obstacles to this total understanding and assimilation.

ACQUIRING ATLANTEAN KNOWLEDGE

The second aspect involves galactic existence, spirit, energy expression, and expanded guidance capabilities. It is to this point that your Age of Aquarius is being guided. The mainstay of learning frequencies for this aspect of evolution is the stimuli of Atlantean knowledge and expressions.

It is in this area that the Love Star crystals can be of the greatest service to you. Their energies are totally implanted with Atlantean knowledge, information that is available to you during this period of time. In addition to using the Love Star crystals, if you will activate your implanted circuitry of etheric crystals and meditate in this state, you will be able to begin to release to consciousness the Atlantean knowledge that is within the recesses of your mind.

In all aspects of development and evolution, the key is the further utilization of the power of your brain and the control of its expression. You must begin to reach out into your galaxy and become aware of sensations, feelings, and energies of existence. This must become a reality for you, not just words that you read on printed pages. You must begin to establish relationships with galactic souls and ask questions of them. You must keep abreast of events that take place at that level. All that is required to achieve this is to be aware of energies that come to you. Feel the sensations of experience, even if you cannot interpret them. In time you will.

THE FINAL GROWTH PROCESS

The third aspect involves universal acceptance, truth, and service. This is the final growth process before one can "reach beyond" and experience All that is. These souls constitute the Hierachy of Universal Spirit, and are responsible for the continuing development of all galactic souls.

I, known on Earth as Pythagoras, have completed my contribution to this dissertation. Before I sever the connection to Adamis, these are words to be shared with you.

Never before in the history of the planet Earth, have opportunities for the fulfillment of mankind been greater than they are at this time. The future of your World is in your hands, and your minds. Your science is still in its infancy, but if you will open your minds to the intangible, yet real, truth of your Universe, together you will achieve the realities of existence.

Within your galaxy are almost one-hundred-million civilizations. Even if you can become aware of ten, you are making great progress in the acceptance of universal existence. Use your heritage wisely, but use it. Draw upon your soul and its past expressions to increase your conscious knowledge. Seek out your sisters and brothers, and unite together to bring fulfillment to mankind.

I am yours within the geometrics of existence.

We are Adamis.

THE REMAINING DIVISIONS OF ENERGY

In earlier discussions, Pythagoras began the explanation of the seven main divisions of energy that comprise your Universe, Ramtos. He has discussed the frequency of "Love." We are going to complete this explanation.

The remaining six divisions are:

1. Karmic Expression

The Atlantean Elders had a saying, "We are beyond all karma. We are not involved with the vibrations that bind and constrict us to universal ties of experience. We are here only to serve."

Universal Law states that the soul eternally endures the experiences of evolution and development. No soul, even the highest Master, exists without new experiences. What is an experience, My Children? It is exposure to new levels of truth. It is exposure to new knowledge, actions, and results. The fundamental basics of karmic expression is created by the polarity of the universal energy grid systems. You refer to this as "cause and effect."

Within the quadrant structure known as the "Tree of Life," we find the perfect example of this system. Each descending level of soul development is attached to the higher level. When one reaches the newly created soul, the chain is complete. All higher levels are then aware of every action and vibration that the new soul experiences. From this experience, all evolve, even the source of the quadrant energies. Remember, evolution is the result of absorption of the energies of an experience.

The most common block to this absorption is the expression of ego. No one is above anything; one is just more aware at that given moment. The result of this expression of denial calls forth the energies of resistance, which lock you into what you have denied.

This befell many of the Atlantean Elders. In truth, many of them were highly evolved souls, there for great contributions to the evolution of the planet. However, as it is during your current times, individual soul growth is paramount and comes before anything else. This is not a statement of selfishness or lack of concern for others. It is Universal Law. It is part of the soul progression established by God.

Each of your souls have evolved through the results of experiences. Each of your souls has achieved a degree of assimilation into a level of soul progression and hierachy. This is the result of the link established between your soul and the Order of the quadrant Tree of Life.

Here you are, on your planet Earth. You are surrounded by chaos and closed minds. What are you supposed to do? The answer is to grow, always to grow. Only in that manner will others be exposed to and experience your soul.

The caste systems of Atlantis is no longer valid for

mankind. The "super races," the clones, the genetic aberrations of "refinement" are not in Universal Order. Atlantis is with you, not the Atlantis that was, but the one that will be. What was is never good enough, if you have grown. Let your Atlantis be a further evolution of what was, and learn from your past experiences and errors.

The power of magnetics is the power of Order. Its prime function is the restoring of balance, always balance. Whenever you have allowed yourself an expression that is not in balance, use your crystals as you have been directed, to correct the infraction and restore you to your truth.

The Elders knew that the effects of every action moved as a chain reaction throughout the Universe. You cannot hide from an experience or action. The results of it are everywhere, and they affect all souls. Remember this, please. You are not ever isolated from the Univese. It is aware and senses everything that is part of your existence.

2. Divine Order

To define Divine Order, one must be Divine Order. To be Divine Order is to be one with the existence of God. We could call it a plan, a plan of a Universe to be created, to evolve and mature, to wane and pass out of existence. We could call it the evolution of a soul from its creation until it becomes one with God.

Sometimes, the closed minds of mankind create their own "divine order"—the accumulation of money, power, greed, control, etc. They become gods to themselves. This negative expression affects everyone. It turns the minds of those who are unsure of themselves, and they become followers.

The course of your patterns of incarnation on the planet Earth are designed to make you aware of the Divine Order of this Universe. You have free will, and yet you have none at all. You have choice, acceptance, rejection, and yet you have none of them. You, the conscious being, are merely the physical expressive instrument of your soul. You exist, and yet you are an illusion at the same time.

The Atlantean Elders knew of eternal life. They knew that they could walk in physical form for hundreds of years. Some of them did, but the majority fell victim to their own "divine order." You, reading these words and absorbing these vibrations, are you locked into your own divine order? Have you found the strength to acknowledge that you are merely a part of all that is and ever will be?

In the course of the evolution of the soul, it becomes aware that it is part of this Order. It has no ego, it has no personal goals or desires. It is part of everything that is. Can you bring yourself to accept this as a reality for yourself? Can you, as Atlantean souls, release the past, allow it to have been, and move forward? Put your minds into your magnetic Universe, and knowledge and peace will enter your hearts.

3. The Fulfillment of God

No soul can experience fulfillment until it has been achieved by God. One can only experience through its Creator. Whenever a person denies God, God does not "grow." Whenever a person leaves his path or is not in service, God is denied growth.

These are the Universal Laws of cause and effect. God has caused your soul to exist, and through your nourishment of evolution, God grows. Let every soul understand and know that, in achieving its growth, it is serving God. The scale of soul progression is constant and firm. There are no variations. Each of you must evolve through the normal levels of progression, level by level, until your soul begins to serve as a Creator. Only then can God be "fulfilled."

4. The "Alone" of Existence

In assisting to achieve the fulfillment of God, there is a conflicting vibration called "aloneness." My Children, you walk on Earth with all of your free will and emotions and yet you sometimes feel all alone. The more you grow, the more alone you feel. Sometimes you feel that you are totally apart from your society and cannot relate to it any longer. This is not in Order for you. If this is true, then what causes this increasing feeling to fall upon you. The reality of growth should bring the feeling of oneness, not aloneness, as you experience.

This feeling comes over you out of your comparisons with others. You grow and, in your growth, decide that you are now different from others, and therefore alone. The more you become aware of your identity, the greater the comparison, and the more alone you feel. In truth, you are alone, alone in the sense of being unique as a soul, for none other is exactly as you are. That is where it ends. The rest are emotional reactions that hamper your service, your acceptance of yourself and others as part of All.

Throughout the history of mankind, you have said that great men and women always walk alone. They are misunderstood, ridiculed, and even called insane. Somehow, they manage to survive and accomplish their purposes. How do they do this? They do not isolate themselves from others. They stand firm in their beliefs and allow others to become part of their truths. God allows you to become part of Its truth if you will only acknowledge your aloneness in its proper expression.

The Atlantis of the future must be one of understanding, based on the acceptance of each being as possessing a soul that is "alone" to itself, and yet an integral part of all other souls.

5. Physical and Spiritual Unity

When the soul and the consciousness have blended their "minds" into one, a unity has occurred. The aloneness of each has been placed into the proper perspective, and the search for universal brotherhood has begun. This is the ultimate aim of the soul, to achieve universal brotherhood through awareness.

If mankind follows in the steps of the Elders, it will not reach its goals. It is mainly for this reason that you must release all thoughts and actions relating to past Atlantean karmic conditions as soon as possible. The longer you hold onto them, the greater the tendency to fall into the same traps once again.

Physical incarnation is not a form of punishment. It is an opportunity for soul advancement and growth. You are not here as a result of something that occurred in the past as a negative expression. You are here for evolution. As each day passes, you will become more aware of past Atlantean experiences. Use them for knowledge and growth, not for punishment and self-recrimination.

All of you have presented your souls in many physically forms. You have served aboard ship, on other planets, and in other galaxies. In each condition, there have been errors generated. If you carry them with you, your soul suffers from the energy blocks that arise. If you try to understand them and learn from them, they can be effective tools for evolution and unity between mind and soul.

Whenever one consciously expresses his ego to the point where it blocks out the awareness of the soul, aloneness occurs. All sense of purpose and unity become distorted, and the energies of power and self-adornment begin to control the life. This has happened throughout the existence of civilizations on Earth. Now it is time for it to end, once and for all time.

6. The Expression as "God"

The magnetic exploration of the soul's existence creates a functional awareness of the position of all souls. The soul loses all sense of insecurity, unworthiness, and adoration in relation to God. Each soul relates to two Gods—the One within and the One that is all encompassing.

In the separation of physical and spiritual unity, there is conflict. The soul is in perspective, and the emotions are confused in adoration and unworthiness. The unity between the magnetic and love vibrations are kept apart, instead of blended.

The Elders who caused the destruction of Atlantis broke this unity. They concentrated on the expression of magnetics and forgot about their relationship with every other soul in existence. Each soul is God, and God is each soul. This must be totally accepted at the conscious level if the Age of Enlightenment is to come to pass—no expression of ego or unworthiness, just acceptance and peace. Then the work can truly be completed, and evolution will progress.

THE TRIANGULATION OF EXPRESSION

Each of these seven vibrational expressions are part of the mathematical triangulation of expression. Each has one "leg" of the triangle as a "leg" of another. They are all interrelated, and lead from one to the other. As one passes from one to another, the power of reaction increases in mathematical progression, and the soul evolves. Each triangulation draws on the strength and the power of the others. This is what creates unity, and total understanding of universal existence and purpose for the soul.

11

This is Adamis.

*Before mankind is able to relate to the coming
awareness of galactic and universal civilizations,
it must accept its own planetary brotherhood.*

*Each of you is like a crystal, brilliant and
without flaws. From time to time, you allow the
clouds of indecision, fear, andjudgment to
penetrate your clarity and distort the
amplification of you Love.*

ELEVATED SOULS ON EARTH

The Atlantean Elders are walking among you. The
Disciples of the Master Jesus, the avatars, the prophets
and seers are walking among you. Heed their presence,
for they are here to lead you back into the brilliance of
God's Light.

Never before have so many souls of elevated status
incarnated on the planet Earth at one time. They are
here to serve as the Shepherds for God. They are here
once again to lead the "lost sheep" through the deserts
into the mansions of the Lord.

Are you one of those Shepherds? Are you one of the chosen 144,000 souls here to lead this planet into the Aquarian Age? Are you here to serve mankind, or to be served? Are you here under karmic responsibility, or to help others understand how to relieve karmic responsibility?

Seek the answers to these questions by looking inside to your soul. Therein lies the source of your eternal existence and the truth of your expression as part of the human race at this time.

It does not matter if you believe in the existence of the physical Atlantis or not. All that matters are the energies and the knowledge that can be utilized by mankind now and in the future.

The Age of Aquarius is the Age of Magnetics and Mathematics, as well as the Age of God's Love. The use of quartz crystals for health, education, and communication, in achieving these goals, cannot be stressed too greatly.

The ability to energize your physical structure and maintain the polarity of your physical organs will, in time, eliminate all forms of "dis-ease." This will enable you to extend the duration of your life cycle on Earth.

STRESS AND ENERGY BLOCKAGE POINTS

There are six main stress and energy blockage points within the physical body.

1. The Throat Chakra

Blockage of the throat chakra is caused by conscious refusal to speak one's truth. It is caused by sacrificing one's needs to make another feel better, to avoid arguments, and it produces a feeling of unworthiness. *Reaction: fear.*

2. The Physical Heart

Blockage of the physical heart signifies the inability to love yourself and to accept yourself exactly as you are. You create "walls" around your heart to protect yourself from you, as well as from others. After all, if someone cannot sense who you are, how can they reject you. *Reaction: anger.*

3. Your Heart Chakra

Blockage of the heart chakra, located in the center of your chest, indicates you have deemed yourself unworthy of your soul, and certainly unworthy of God. You have "sinned." You have committed all forms of adultery. You do not like yourself, for you have compared yourself to others. *Reaction: emptiness.*

4. The Solar Plexus Chakra

Blockage of the solar plexus chakra, located beneath the rib cage, connotes the area of acceptance, the focus of ingestion and dissemination of all knowledge and rections to your body. You are not willing to take a chance on yourself, to risk being wrong; therefore you hold all of it in place to lie fallow and maintain existing insecurities. *Reaction: anxiety.*

5. The Spleen Chakra

Blockage of the spleen chakra, located three inches below the navel, involves the gateway to your emotional and sensual expressions. The conditioning of unworthiness manifests itself. Do you want to acknowledge yourself as a beautiful creation and to express emotions? You want to deny the existence of the balance of your truth in relation to your soul. *Reaction: feeling threatened.*

6. The Base Chakra

Blockage of the base chakra, which is the seat of emotional expression, indicates the conditioning of shame, unworthiness, judgment of self, and lack of understanding of functions. *Reactions: cold, anxiety, mistrust.*

CRYSTAL APPLICATIONS TO RELIEVE BLOCKAGES

To eliminate one or all of these blocks to someone's happiness and fulfillment, we recommend the following crystal applications.

Place clear, single-terminated quartz crystals, approximately one and one-half inches long, on all the subject's problem areas, all points upward. Pass the paddles* of pastel rose and of green over the body in a circular motion for five minutes. When this has been completed, place one hand on the heart chakra and send Love energy into the entire body.

This treatment will open the energy circuitry between the blocked areas and allow for emotional healing to take place. It is recommended that the treatment be repeated on a weekly basis for four weeks. If a blockage persists, place two crystals on that area to intensify the energy and the blockage will be removed.

In order for you to unite consciously with your soul, all judgments of self must be removed. You must recognize the Temple of your soul, your physical body. You

---

*See footnote on page 66.

must honor it and use it as a true expression of the sharing of Love, for that is the purpose for its creation.

The coming of the Age of Aquarius has brought with it the energies of decision. In the past, many have elected to remain in a noncommittal frame of mind, waiting to have the actions of others determine their courses of action. Now, this complacency can no longer be maintained. Because of this, many have found themselves living in untruth and do not know how to change their attitudes.

This situation has led to the need for additional forms of cleansing of the physical body, as the individual's immune or truth system is being affected. Please remember that, as long as mankind will declare itself imperfect, it will create imperfections.

TREATING CONDITIONS OF "UNTRUTH"

The treating of conditions caused by this type of "untruth" requires the trinity of energy expressions—color, sound, and vibrations.

Place the person on his back in a prone position in a pattern of twelve single-terminated crystals. Place additional crystals on top of the body in the following positions, all pointing upwards, twelve crystals in all:

- On the third eye chakra
- On the throat chakra
- On each shoulder
- On the heart chakra
- On the navel
- In the palm of each hand
- On the top of each thigh
- On the top of each ankle

This pattern opens the complete energy network to the magnetic vibrations of the crystals. Take the purple and blue paddles, one in each hand, and move them over the entire body in circular motions. (It does not matter in which direction you move the paddles.) Begin to chant the persons first name as you move the paddles over the body Soon you will sense a change in your vocal tones. Allow this to happen, and continue to chant.

Continue this treatment for five minutes, and then rest for ten minutes. Repeat the treatment once more.

When the treatment has been completed, allow the person to rest for at least twenty minutes before moving. This will permit the energy to condition the body and prepare it for changes that may occur.

This application is the beginning of total spiritual healing treatments as they were conducted in ancient Atlantis. Some may have assumed that the Atlanteans wee too advanced to be open to serious physical ailments, but this is not true. Whenever anyone is exposed to conditions of free-will expression, conditions of negativity and self-judgment can be manifested through physical imperfections.

ATLANTEAN AND UNIVERSAL SYMBOLS

As the planet Earth moves into Atlantean consciousness, mankind will become aware of the language of geometrics. This is a form of communication and expression that cannot be distorted nor emotionally misinterpreted.

We will present you with a series of Atlantean and universal symbols that are part of this language. Some of you will feel familiar with these forms. If this is the case, meditate on the symbols to bring forth greater clarity and interpretation for yourself.

Expansion

The following represents pure energy. It is forceful and pointed in areas, showing strength and determination, and yet soft and fluid. It symbolizes expansion.

Low Level Growth

Notice that there seems to be a "child" within this symbol. It is contained by a soft, flowing outer shell of energy that allows it to be nurtured. This is a symbol of development, of growth at a low level, and of protection during that growth to shield it from negativity.

Atlantean Energies

This can be interpreted as either a bolt of energy or the ladder of growth. Both interpretations are applicable. It is used to stimulate and relate to the energies of the ancient Atlantean era.

Rising to Spiritual Stability

This symbol, although purely geometric in construction, appears to be fluid in movement. It is composed of several fluid triangles, larger at the bottom and becoming more clearly defined at the top. It symbolizes a rising from the Earth to the spiritual stability that leads to freedom from lower restrictions.

Protection from Negative Expression

A symbol of abstraction, flowing and yet restricted, this following is used as a protection from negative expression and to augment the balance of your energy meridians.

Karmic Balance

In the following, notice that there is a triangle at the top left and a triangle at the lower right, with an abstraction in the middle. This is the total expression of balance of karmic vibrations and experiences. It tells one to experience all sides before determining truth.

A Catalyst

In the following, the circle and the triangle are at opposite ends, with fluidity in the center. The center unites the rigid opposition of extremes. It symbolizes a catalytic reaction between people and situations.

Obstacles

This is the symbol of Earth power and obstacles to overcome. The path to the apex is not smooth, unless one walks around and looks at the other side. It means that, many times, a path that seems to be full of obstacles is not necessarily the one to pursue. You have to pursue it only when you believe that you must suffer.

Perils

This symbol is open-ended. It portrays two caverns or pits that one may fall into, and the perils that one may face during the course of life. In another sense, it offers the protection and shelter from negativity and oppression, knowing that one can rise at will, for one is always free.

God

Within these energies are the total male and female expression—the energies of raw power and of soft love. The Earth plane is symbolized by the horizontal, and the spiritual plane by the vertical. The symbol relates to God, all knowing, wise and benevolent.

Power

This is a symbol of power. You could compare the extended points to the energy of the human aura, extending itself and then drawing back, always flexible. It signifies learning, helping to remove restrictions and limitations from ones' concepts of thinking and from ones' life.

Choice

This figure appears as a three-petaled flower, open at the bottom to allow the energy from Mother Nature to surge through, so that it may open, expand, and bloom. As it grows, it becomes taller and taller until it reaches the spiritual realms. This is a symbol of choice. Exposure has been achieved; now it is time for decision— to grow or to wither.

Maternal Guidance

These energies are soft yet firm. They symbolize maternal guidance. They have the capacity to rule and share with love, but also with firmness, to guide into the proper direction. They tell you to be strong in your truth, but always with love.

Balancing

It should be obvious to the eye that the following has the ability to change shape at any moment without breaking. It can always maintain the balance inside the core. It tells us to relate to both sides of a situation, not to be strict and rigid.

Self-Control

This is our symbol of symmetry and can be symmetrical if necessary. It is a symbol of self-control and self-direction of actions and expressions. You cannot reach your goals without these qualities.

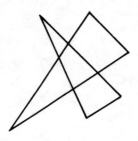

Power of the Physical Plane

This symbol relates power as applied to the physical plane. Energy enters through the top and builds a larger and larger foundation of strength and truth to relate to. It utilizes growth to assist nature in its evolution.

Conscious Control

This is a symbol of expression of the infinite ability to relate to the simple as well as the complex. It is a symbol of conscious control, to allow for assimilation of concepts, ideas, and growth. It says to take a chance on yourself.

Eternal Flow

This is a symbol of eternal flow. It is open at all ends and never closes, for the lines continue and extend onward eternally. It tells one not to sit on past glories and past performances. If you ever say, "I know what I need to know," use these energies to move forward.

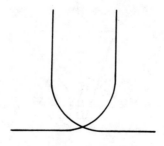

Physical Achievement

The following shapes are significant in that they reflect the adaptation of spiritual vibrations to enable them to be compatible in the physical world. The symbol relates to physical achievement, utilizing spiritual wealth.

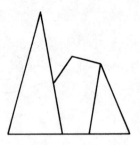

Power of the Initiate

This is the symbol of the power of the initiate, containing flow and motion. It says to place all in perspective to prepare for final truth.

Acceptance

The symbol of acceptance. The knowing of the weight and the might in the arms, and of the power that one possesses. At the same time, one knows that the power must be used with care and tenderness, for it can be destructive as well.

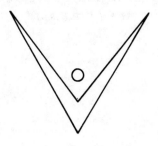

Eternal Fulfillment

This contains all the energies of Creation. It is a symbol of eternal fulfillment and achievement. It tells you to accept the eternity of your soul as a child of God.

These symbols have not been consciously viewed for many thousands of years. The time has come when mankind has once again reached the place where it is able to assimilate these vibrations.

Let all strive to continue to grow and make yourselves worthy of the Love that is available to all mankind.

12

This is "Strength" from Atlantis.

The trilogy of expression pertaining to the ancient and modern-day civilizations of Atlantis is coming to completion. I speak for all of those who have shared their evolution and energies with you when I say that it has been the pleasure of spirit to be a contributing factor to the increased human awareness and stimulation of mind that, it is hoped, will lead to your evolution. If this is accomplished, then our purpose will have been fulfilled.

DECISIONS

Mankind is on the brink of a great awakening of consciousness, and it is in Order for you to place yourselves into your unity of expressions as rapidly as possible. It is in Order for you to place yourself among those Children of God who are still consciously asleep, so that you may open their minds to their souls.

Your Era of Enlightenment is with you now, and whether it achieves fulfillment or not is totally within your hands and your hearts. Before this cycle, your year of 1985, has come to completion, you must make up your mind and come to your decision. You must either accept your role upon the planet Earth as one of service or deny it. Either decision will benefit mankind, for it will remove one more disturbing frequency of indecision from your atmosphere.

We, "Strength," are always available to serve. If it comes to your mind that you have a need for our knowledge and past experience, place the thought of us in your mind, and if our frequencies are compatible, we shall be with you.

We look forward to sharing with you again
in the future. Blessings upon you.

This is Adamis speaking.

THE WORK AHEAD

The utilization of the quartz crystals in the application and conduct of your lives from this point forward is of the utmost importance for you. As we have said to you in the past, it is within your best interests to remember always that they are tools of your expression, that you are not to become dependent upon them and use them as a crutch. In that manner, they will continue to serve you well.

The work ahead for mankind involves the opening of the minds of those of God's Children who are still sleeping. This must be done in order to enable them to retain their compatibility with the frequencies of your Age of Enlightenment. This will also enable their souls to return to the planet Earth for future growth and evolution.

So we charge you with the task of serving your sisters and brothers who have need for you. And we charge you with the task of releasing all constricting vibrations that you bear around your neck as chains of weight. Cast them aside, for you no longer have a need for them. Stand tall, with your shoulders square and your head erect, and acknowledge the unity of yourself. Acknowledge the understanding of the placement of God within the life expression.

LEARN FROM ATLANTIS

There is much for you to learn from your ancient Atlantean heritage. Set the condition in your mind that all knowledge that comes to you will be used for positive actions, and the awareness of negative actions will be transmuted so that they need not occur again in the future. Do not sit in your meditations and take yourself back to ancient Atlantean times. Stay where you are, and bring the energies of the past to the present. Let them be with you in the Now. This will give you the clarity and understanding within your own frequencies, and will always enable you to be totally in control.

The Atlantean civilizations were neither all good nor all bad. For the most part, it was a most positive expression. The pictures that We have painted for you at various times were not intended to cast aspersions upon this civilization. They were presented so that you should not live in romantic illusions, so that you should not look upon any expression as the ultimate to achieve. Within most things there are flaws, and the flaws represent the opportunity for growth. Recognize them as such, and grow from their expression. Do not allow them to draw you into their essence.

Take the words that We have shared with you and explore them to the greatest depths. Try to begin to understand what is known as an Atlantean consciousness. It does not pertain to one set of conditions and circumstances. It has been here before Earth, and it will be here after Earth has fulfilled its service and existence. You are dealing with a state of awareness. You are dealing with a state of incentives, of evolution, and—most of all—with the understanding of the seven energy aspects of your Universe, the total blending of magnetics and love frequencies of God. It has been to this purpose that all has been served and has occurred.

We strongly suggest that time and effort be expended in the area of solidifying the etheric crystaline structure inside of your physical bodies. The more you activate these centers, the greater the amplification, the more you will be able to achieve for yourself and for mankind.

The majority of information that is needed for you for the future is stored within the magnetic frequencies of the Universe. The only method by which this information can be released to you is through your own compatibility with these magnetic frequencies. The process of meditation and mental activation of these centers will help you to accomplish this goal.

What lies ahead for the future of mankind in the New Atlantean Era—scientific inventions, the total utilization of the speed of thought process for travel, for altering pure energy into physical matter, for communication with other worlds and other civilizations that exist within your Universe.

ACHIEVING ONENESS

Achieving the Oneness and the acceptance of universal existence will give every being upon the planet Earth the confidence and the incentive to create one World here upon your planet Earth. Unity will come to pass, and with the unity and the peace, many of the separations between mankind will fall away. Religious differences, racial concerns, sexual preferences will no longer be of importance for you. All will be aware that each individual is experiencing his choice, and will help him understand in his evolution another facet of construction and existence. Peace and brotherhood will come to reign on the planet Earth.

Those souls who have chosen not to grow, who have elected to pursue the course of their expression in an emotional pattern, will, when their present expression has been completed, incarnate elsewhere. For no soul is denied its choice and method of growth, and all will retain compatibility with planets' frequencies.

Those who have advanced their evolution will return to the planet Earth. Here they will become part of this New Age of Expression and Knowledge. In time, your planet of Earth will become a planet of service for your solar system. It will be a mainstay of knowledge and energy that lower forms of civilization may draw upon. This is the progression of Order. One is always in the service of others.

If there is but one area of information that can assist you in the development and evolution of your existence, let it be the area concerning relationships with yourself and with others. Look around you, notice how, even at this time, your system of relationships has greatly altered itself. Your freedom of expression, your insisting upon your rights to have friends of both sexes without them being a threat, is with you. Draw upon the method of associations from ancient Atlantis. Create your unions out of compatibilities at the deepest levels you can be aware of, the levels that are not consciously obvious to others, but that enter your heart in a silent manner of peace and knowing.

THE CHILDREN

Most important of all, look to your children. They are the future. Try to understand that the souls of your children have not come here for the same functions that your soul entered. The souls of your children are here to achieve higher forms of expression and service. Because of this fact, your responsibility to them is greater than your parents' responsibility to you. Without exception, always keep in the forefront of your mind all of the trials and obstacles that you endured as a child, all of the pain and the aloneness that you experienced, and do not allow this to occur for your children. Accept the fact that they are not here to experience these lessons. They are here in service to unite mankind, and the earlier the years that they begin their work, the sooner all will come to pass.

Pay heed to the area of this book pertaining to children and their use of crystals. It is most important for them. It will provide them with the strength to stand tall, in spite of all the opposition that they will receive from their peers who are still asleep.

KNOW WHO YOU ARE

For you, allow yourself the acknowledgment of who you are. Allow yourself to be an integral part of your society. Do not create a separation between yourself and others, for this is where your work is. Whenever mankind has divided itself into categories, stating that some are better than others, that one society is more advanced than others, wars have resulted.

There can no longer be separation of societies. There can no longer be comparisons of cultures and methods of expression. There can only be acceptance of all, and with the acceptance comes the integration and sharing of knowledge and progress, so that all mankind will benefit from the results. All fears of oppression and conquest, all competitive natures to place one above another, must be put aside. The understanding that all are the same must be allowed to enter the hearts of all mankind in security, in knowing, and in love. Then your World can become as One, and all mankind will walk linked arm in arm into the Glory and the Light of God.

The energies for this dissertation have been completed. All is in Universal Order. And we conclude with the following dissertation that, it is hoped, will bring into perspective the future course and path of your life's expression.

"AM I A UNIVERSE?"

I am a segment of mankind. I was born of a seed. I grew and matured. I sleep, I eat, I work, I play, I love, and I grow. In my growth, I discover two realities— myself and God. This ripening growth creates an osmosis between the two, and soon I am me. I stand alone, stripped of all adornments, and declare my oneness within myself, and the God within me.

Now it is time for me to transmute my self-love and beliefs into reality. I spread my arms and declare myself a Child of God. My vibrations emanate from my being and form an umbrella of Light and Love. I invite other of God's Children to walk under my umbrella with me. Some find peace and love. Others bless me and walk on. The choice is always theirs.

Those who stay entrust me with their vibrations. I nurture them and encourage them to grow and find their truths. I teach them my truth, and they try it on for size. Sometimes, in their experiences, it is too large, sometimes too small. They learn from taking actions. They slip and fall. They achieve growth and success. They laugh and they cry. They die and are reborn. They bear fruit and are barren.

Slowly but surely, they grow, and their Light begins to shine brighter and brighter. They have suffered in love, altered their reaction patterns, and one day become aware of their identity. They flex their vibrations, and extend a foot outside of my umbrella to allow the rain to sprinkle on them. They begin to teach, to truly learn who they are, to spread and enlarge their truths.

One day, they begin to sense a total awareness and oneness with the God within, and they know it is time to leave and walk alone, yet never alone. They spread their arms and await those seeking to hear their truths and walk under their umbrellas.

A Child is born, experiences, matures, ripens, and becomes an umbrella. An umbrella? A Universe! Am I a Universe! Aren't we all!

Our Blessings upon your souls.

NOTES

NOTES

UNIVERSAL
LAW

for the
Aquarian
Age

DR. FRANK ALPER

UNIVERSAL LAW is a "must have" addition to all of our lives. In simple, easy to understand language we are guided into responsible GOD consciousness.

Universal Law is an expanding vibration, always in motion. Each individual is responsible for his own interpretation of the Law and its application in his life. If after an action has been taken an error has been made, it can be corrected by another action called karma. This constitutes the growth of mankind.

This book presents many topics for the Aquarian Age including:

- **Spiritual Union**
- **Personal Morality**
- **Responsibility to Ego**
- **The Ten Commandments**

Universal Law may be purchased for $9.95 from *ARIZONA METAPHYSICAL SOCIETY*.
Please see our order form at the back of this book.

Dr. Frank Alper

BOOKS
TAPES
LECTURE
SERIES

From
The Arizona Metaphysical Society

EXPLORING ATLANTIS

BOOKS
Volume I $11.95

This is the first volume of a trilogy. Its contents are a
compilation of lectures channeled through the soul of
Dr. Frank Alper. The majority of this book is devoted to the
functions and uses of quartz crystals by the Atlanteans.
Their sizes, shapes, colors and functions are an integral part
of this presentation. Many geometric patterns for healing
with the crystals are described in detail. This book also deals
with the social, moral, sexual and spiritual customs and habits
of the ancient Atlanteans. Additionally, descriptions and
functions of the Great Healing Temple and the Temple
Of The Dolphins are provided in great detail.

Volume II $11.95

This volume is the continued examination of ancient Atlantean
cultures, living patterns and development. It also deals
with the destruction of Atlantis and the causes for its
downfall. There are contained in these pages many
additional aspects pertaining to healing, education and
surgery through the application of quartz crystals.
Approximately sixty specific diseases and the crystal
patterns for alleviating them are described in detail.

Volume III $11.95

This volume completes the final leg of the triangle and
contains a complete picture of the causes and effects
that were created through the existence of ancient Atlantis.
Additional material is presented on healing with crystals,
color, sound, seed and love star crystals and crystal
for the education of children. The energies of The Golden
Triad, Universal Energy Divisions and the future Atlantis
are also discussed. There is also a special chapter dealing
with the Chakras and an extended series of Atlantean and
universal symbols. These symbols are a form of
communication and expression that can not be distorted,
nor emotionally mis-interpreted.

VIDEO $49.95
VHS or BETA available, please specify

A two-hour video "Journey Through Time" with Dr. Frank Alper.
In this unique video cassette, Dr. Alper ties together for
the first time, the moral, social, cultural and economic
practices and philosophies of Ancient Atlantis. He correlates
the priorities that mankind faces today, how we can rise
above destruction and utilize this knowledge to bring
mankind into this age of enlightenment.

HEALING WITH CRYSTALS

VIDEO $49.95
VHS or BETA available, please specify

A Video Program with Dr. Frank Alper showing his healing techniques with crystals.

Dr. Frank Alper has long been considered the pioneer in healing with magnetic energies using geometric configurations. This video tape shows the placement and the way to use crystals for healing as well as the means for giving new energies to the places where they are needed most.

AUDIO CASSETTES
CRYSTALS, COLOR AND SOUND (seven tape set,
6½ hours) $55.00
A taped seminar dealing with crystals, color and sound.

AUDIO CASSETTES

The Atlantean Chants   **$8.00**
Twenty-four chants of ancient Atlantean vibrations that pertain to growth and evolvement.

Murvin—Commander of Jupiter I   **$10.00**
An interview with Murvin, who describes the space brothers, life and purpose aboard ship.

The Twelve Disciples   **$10.00**
Channeled by the energies of Peter and the Father.

Solomon: Universal Consciousness   **$10.00**
How to achieve Universal Consciousness. Includes a guided meditation by Solomon.

Conditioning the Child of Light   **$10.00**
How to survive and relate to society from your spiritual essence.

Success and Failure Mechanisms   **$10.00**
Determine your mind orientation relating to goal achievement and balance.

Removing Emotional and Sexual Blocks   **$10.00**
Tools to help you relive self-imposed blocks that hamper fulfillment.

The Golden Triad   **$10.00**
The energies of the Age of Aquarius. The power of the energies of creative matter.

The Word   **$8.00**
A description of the symbolic twenty-two steps of Karmic evolution.

Universal Law (two tape set)   **$18.00**
Over thirty Universal Laws are channeled and described by the energies of the Father.

The Twelve Initiations (two tape set)   **$18.00**
A description of the physical and spiritual initiations of the soul.

BOOKS

Moses and the Bible (volumes I–IV)   **$11.95**

A spiritual interpretation of Creation and the written word. The Old and New Testaments. Ancient civilizations on and inside the earth, spiritual laws, the Ten Commandments, and much more.

"An Evening With Christos" (volumes I–V)   **$14.95**

A year of monthly spiritual channelings consisting of a lecture, followed by questions and answers. The energies of many masters have contributed to these timeless volumes.

Universal Healing Rays (pamphlet)   **$2.00**

THE CONTINUING TAPE SERIES

Quarterly	**$28.00**
Semi-Annually	**$52.00**
Annually	**$96.00**

The spiritual teachings of Dr. Frank Alper are now available on sixty-minute tapes. Each month you will receive new information for your growth and evolution.

The tapes will contain information pertaining to the new energies of the Aquarian age, coming spiritual awakenings and events, higher interpretations of many basic laws of spiritual life and much more.

This program will enable you to continue your growth in a progressive manner, with new stimuli.

The program may be subscribed to on a quarterly, semi-annual, or annual basis.

PAST SUBJECTS INCLUDE:

Karma, Love & Detachment	Planetary Evolution
Truth & Responsibility	Universal Creation
The Union of Marriage	Male & Female Energies
Spiritual Path vs. Religion	The Initiation of Fire
Learning to Channel	Building Confidence
Coping with Spiritual & Sexual Stress	

Any of the above tapes may be ordered singly   **$10.00 each**

Order Form

	Cost	Qty.
BOOKS		
UNIVERSAL LAW	$ 9.95	
EXPLORING ATLANTIS I II III (Circle Choices)	$11.95 ea.	
EVENING WITH CHRISTOS I II III IV V (Circle Choices)	$14.95 ea.	
MOSES AND THE BIBLE I II III IV (Circle Choices)	$11.95 ea.	
UNIVERSAL HEALING RAYS	$ 2.00	
VIDEO TAPES		
EXPLORING ATLANTIS, VHS or BETA (Circle One)	$49.95	
HEALING WITH CRYSTALS, VHS or BETA (Circle One)	$49.95	
AUDIO CASSETTES		
ATLANTEAN CHANTS	$ 8.00	
MURVIN	$10.00	
TWELVE DISCIPLES	$10.00	
SOLOMON	$10.00	
THE CHILD OF LIGHT	$10.00	
UNIVERSAL LAW (2 tape set)	$18.00	
THE GOLDEN TRIAD	$10.00	
CRYSTALS, COLOR AND SOUND (7 tape set)	$55.00	
TWELVE INITIATIONS (2 tape set)	$18.00	
THE WORD	$ 8.00	
SUCCESS AND FAILURE MECHANISMS	$10.00	
REMOVING EMOTIONAL & SEXUAL BLOCKS	$10.00	
TAPE SERIES		
Quarterly Basis $28.00 Semi-Annually $52.00 Annually $96.00		
INDIVIDUAL TAPES (List your choices on a separate paper)	$10.00 ea.	
SUB TOTAL		
POSTAGE		
TOTAL		

■ **Handling charges applicable to all orders**

$ 0.01 – $10.00	add $1.00
$10.01 – 20.00	add $2.00
$20.01 – 30.00	add $3.00
$30.01 – 50.00	add $4.00
$50.01 – 100.00	add $5.00
$100 and up	add $7.00

Handling charges and prices subject to change without notice.

■ **Canada and Mexico**
Add $1.00 to each printed handling charge

■ **Orders outside of North America.**
For Surface Mail, add ten percent (10%) of your total order to the printed handling charge.
For AIR MAIL, add thirty percent (30%) of your total order to the printed handling charge

■ Please allow 2 – 4 weeks for delivery

■ U.S. funds only

■ No credit cards

Make checks payable to:
Arizona Metaphysical Society
P.O. Box 44027
Phoenix, AZ 85064
(602) 956-1676

Name

Address

City

State   Zip

Phone (   )